Print ISBN: 979-8-35094-912-4

Illustrations and layout by Christa Markley

First printing edition 2024.

For more resources about "teaching from the heart," visit The Spirit of Teaching at www.spiritofteaching.org.

Hear stories from teachers about their professional journeys on the podcast "Teacher Tales," available on all podcast platforms.

DEDICATION

*This book is dedicated to every living human being,
past and present, who has walked the path of life,
learning lessons with each step forward.*

Linda's Camino Journey

BAY of BISCAY

Galicia

Asturias

Castillo & León

ESPAÑA

N

LEÓN

MAZARIFE

ASTORGA

HOSPITAL del ORBIGO

RABANAL de CAMINO

EL ACEBO de SAN MIGUEL

PONFERRADA

VILAFRANCA del BIERZO

HERRERIAS

O'CEBREIRO

TRIACASTELA

SARRIA

PORTOMARÍN

PALAS do REI

MELIDE

ARZUA

AMENAL

SANTIAGO de COMPOSTELA

CONTENTS

PREFACE

THE VALUE OF OUR TRUE SELF

"A bird doesn't sing because it has an answer, it sings because it has a song."

—MAYA ANGELOU, POET & AUTHOR

AFFIRMATION:

I always know what to do when I get still and tune in to the melody and lyrics playing in my heart.

We all have a unique song inside us to sing to the world. Throughout my career as a teacher, I sang every day, both literally and figuratively. My heart sang through the lessons I taught, which had been inspired by the lessons I had learned. My students and I might literally sing a "piggyback song" as inspiration for them to more easily understand and remember a grammar concept in Spanish. Or maybe it was through games, play, and curious exploration into a world of possibilities. Regardless, teaching was always about sharing my truth through heartfelt words, experiences, content and lessons that I had discovered on my personal journey for knowledge and knowing. I wanted to pass on all that I had learned in order to ignite a fire inside my students to learn, grow and discover their own personal truths and how they fit into this world of possibilities. Learning was all about the personal experience, the joy and the journey, and not so focused on a prescribed set of answers as "one size fits all." This was always my intention, my greatest achievement and my most loving gift to them.

Like most teachers, I felt a calling to teach and make a difference in the world... all for the greater good! Teaching is a heart-centered profession, yet in today's education environment the teacher's heart is getting broken again, and again, and again. Feelings of being lost, confused, controlled, disempowered, uninspired, and devalued have extinguished the once-blazing fires of passion and the heartfelt calling to teach and make a difference in the world. As a result, teachers are leaving the profession in droves. Not only that, but the number of young people becoming education majors in college is down 42 percent. I thought the educational crisis was peaking several years ago as I watched my dear friends and colleagues leave a career that they thought they would be in forever...including me! Well, it is just getting worse with teacher shortages being the highest ever and teacher morale at its lowest point. The dispiriting and terrifying experience of classroom teaching throughout the COVID-19 pandemic only worsened the situation.

During my career of 35-plus years, I experienced many passes of the educational pendulum swinging back and forth. There were always highs and lows, but nothing like the extremes we are experiencing today. The negative "spirit" that permeates the classroom is overwhelming as teachers and students struggle to cope and protect their fragile human hearts from judgment, rejection, disempowerment, and shame. Fear is the foundation of the curriculum and feelings of "not enough" are the standards by which we all live.

In recent years, I have witnessed the once-loving and nurturing energy in the classroom become toxic, not because teachers or students or administrators are bad, but because the system is flawed by an overwhelming negativity driven from a place of "lack" instead of abundance, a mentality of "not enough" instead of "not yet," and a spirit of competition instead of community. What seems to be "accountability" is really coming from a place of "gotcha" with the intention of getting rid of all the "bad" elements.

I left the profession with my own broken heart, lost on my journey and dispirited by all that I was seeing and feeling about my beloved vocation (from Latin *vocare*, to call). Without the light of my calling to guide me, I was left in the darkness with only questions. Had I failed or just fallen from grace? If not a classroom teacher, then who was I, and what was my purpose? How was I ever going to mend and heal my broken heart so that I could once again answer my calling and let the light of my passion shine brightly? Would I ever again be able to share my love song of learning through the spirit of curiosity, self discovery, connections, and service to the greater good of humanity?

The answers to these essential life questions, as always, came in the form of lessons. I had spent my whole life carefully crafting lesson plans for my students that would spark their curiosity and take them step-by-step on a personalized learning journey to help them find meaning and direction. Well, that's exactly what the Universe planned for me, and it came in the form of walking halfway across Spain on the ancient pilgrim trail of the Camino de Santiago. On the Camino, in the footsteps of millions of "peregrinos" across centuries, there were no quick answers, no multiple choice selections or true/false solutions that were "one size fits all."

Like any true and meaningful lesson in life, we are given multiple opportunities to figure things out, one step at a time. We all become confused, lost, stumble, and fall. And we never really achieve mastery or perfection, contrary to what we are taught in school. That is the gift of being human and the real treasure of the learning journey of life. It is all about the lessons and the questions we choose to ask in order to become more aware of the choices that will empower us and move us along our learning path to discover our love song and our passion that we will share with the world. It is not so much about the answers as it is about the questions we choose to ask and the reflection of ourselves that we see in them.

Life is a journey of lessons. There is no test, no failure, no right answer, no curriculum. The only standards are the ones that come from the true spirit of our common humanity. We are forever teachers and students on this learning journey of life. My hope is that by sharing some of my life lessons as a teacher and a student, I can help support and inspire others on their learning journey of curiosity, self-discovery, connections, reflection, and enlightenment so that they too might find their song and share it with the world.

So, this is my learning journey and the lessons that led me back home to my true spirit. This is my love song to the child in each of us who falls down, gets lost, confused, frustrated, afraid and overwhelmed, but who is just trying to figure things out, step-by-step, one lesson at a time, to find their way in the world!

"Don't die with your music inside of you."
—WAYNE DYER, AUTHOR & SPEAKER

LEARNING LESSONS

Reader's Guide

The purpose of this book is to share my journey of learning lessons on my path in life, both in and out of the classroom. I hope that the reader will be inspired not only to go on a journey of personal reflection, but also to make some interpersonal connections to deepen their learning and lead them to their next step forward on their path in life.

Like on the pilgrim's path of the Camino de Santiago, each chapter will share a part or "stage", as you will, of my path in life and the lessons I learned that then led me to the next "stage."

Each chapter will have an inspirational quote as well as a mantra that is connected to the lesson and theme of that chapter. At the end of each chapter, I have provided two activities for you:

Personal Reflection Activity, an activity meant for you to look inward, reflecting on what you have learned and your "takeaway" from that learning.

Interpersonal Connection Activity, an activity that may or may not be done with another person. The intention is to take what you have learned from your Personal Reflection Activity and, metaphorically, hold it up as a "mirror" for teaching and learning with another person.

Through these two types of experiences in life, we learn the lessons that we are meant to learn so that we can grow into the next best version of ourselves. With each lesson and step forward, we tap into the pieces of ourselves that help us to expand, extend, and eventually, exfoliate the layers of ignorance that hold us back.

As human beings, we are constantly presented with learning opportunities that will challenge us, frustrate us, and even push us to anger or tears. At the same time, we are also presented with learning opportunities that will excite us, inspire us, and move us into a more well-rounded and "whole" human being. But learning isn't linear. On our journey, we can sometimes lose our way and struggle to find a path forward. We spend all our time and energy trying to recover the "lost" pieces of ourselves so that we can feel whole again.

Learning lessons starts from the day we are born and continues until the day we die. So, as long as we are learning lessons…both the hard, unpleasant ones as well as the easy, pleasant ones, we should remember to be grateful and open to all the learning opportunities that present themselves to us because there is always a lesson to learn—and a lesson to share.

We are all in this learning journey called "life" together. We are all both students and teachers, holding hands and taking that next brave step forward toward our next greater understanding in the bigger picture in order to find out place and purpose in it.

So take a deep breath, grab a journal or notebook, and take my hand as we journey through *Learning Lessons* together.

Buen Camino, pilgrim!

1

DATA, GRADES AND CHECKLISTS

"Let it go."

— FROZEN

AFFIRMATION:

I am enough.

As I was called to the counter of the next worker at the Pilgrim's Office in Santiago de Compostela, I felt a flutter of butterflies swirling around in my stomach as if I were stepping out on a stage to give a presentation. I never really have felt nervous being in front of a crowd of people doing a presentation. It is what teachers do every day I suppose. It wasn't the achy feeling I had been having for the past three days since my "illness." Instead, it was a feeling of tickling in my tummy like a bunch of butterflies being released and set free. No longer a chrysalis. No more "bug juice," as Sue Monk Kidd calls it. A metamorphosis had taken place, and a newfound freedom of my soul had emerged.

There was a long line and plenty of time to reflect before it was my turn, not that I hadn't been doing that for the past month while I walked halfway across Spain! How had I gotten here, figuratively speaking? What had led me to travel to a different continent to walk 15-20 miles per day on an ancient religious path called the Camino Francés? Like most of the peregrinos (pilgrims), I was seeking answers to life's big questions: Who am I? and What is my purpose? We are born into this world, are given a name and sent along a path of learning and self-discovery. We go to school and are shown all the "right" answers to all the "right" questions. We are conditioned to believe that life is like school and that we should always have the right answers. But what if we don't? What if somehow along the way, we get off path, and we are lost? What if we allow things outside of ourselves to define who we are and set our path instead? What will happen if we don't have all the "right" answers and we are frozen in fear to make a choice because we are afraid of being wrong, or that we will be shamed, or made fun of, or that we will fall short as the end results are not enough? Or rather... we are not enough?

So, as I stood in line waiting to be called to my final exam, my summative assessment of the Camino, I found myself using all my background knowledge and personal experiences as a context in which to make meaning of such a "simple" inquiry. There were only three short questions they were going to ask me at the Pilgrim's Office.

Question 1.

"What is your name?" Well, that's easy... Or was it? "What's in a name?" said Shakespeare. Other languages, such as Romance languages like French and Spanish, express this as "what do you call yourself?" Here we can substitute many labels for name-calling, and with all with judgment behind them. We can substitute titles like Mr., Mrs., Miss, Director, or Doctor, and feel empowered and better than others, or smaller and disempowered by others. A seemingly simple question like this now had such a deeper meaning than it had before I started the Camino.

Question 2.

"Where are you from?" This question begs the exploration of so many beliefs, from those about our family origin, to our

DNA origin, to our origin from the Divine and how we fit in to the bigger picture of humanity. We like to add details, sometimes stereotypes, to build context and connection. Like with our name, we identify greatly with our origin and the culture associated with that place. I'm from Green Bay, and I'm a Packers fan. I'm from the country and love having a lot of land and few neighbors. I'm from up North, down South, out West… My family is Italian, and we are really loud and boisterous. My family is originally from England and came over shortly after the Mayflower. There are so many labels to choose from.

"Well, this is easy so far," I thought. What an easy "test!" I expected something much more profound and personal. The first two questions, I couldn't get wrong. There was only one right answer for each one, right? And the third one was technically multiple choice, so I had a 50/50 chance of getting it "right," right? But that was totally not true.

Question 3.

"What was your purpose for doing the Camino…spiritual or religious?" I had so many answers now and very few questions! My soul was once again intact. I had learned so much, and my journey on the Camino had changed me forever. Did they not want to know anything about that? Each pilgrim has a different, unique and interesting story. Aren't they curious to hear about everyone's learning journey? Their questions and approach were hitting someplace deep inside me.

Why would they make such a profound, meaningful question multiple choice with only two possibilities? Moreover, if each pilgrim's experience and purpose could be narrowed down and put into two boxes, why didn't they at least then give the pilgrim an opportunity to explain? I understand that time is an issue, but weren't they interested in finding out just a little about each person's journey? In three words, three sentences, three minutes? Just something that would initiate reflection and solidify the learning journey that had taken place. I had learned and grown so much more than what could ever be reflected in my three short answers.

·   ·   ·

As a language teacher, I've learned and taught a lot about communication. I know that there are actually three modes of communication. It starts with the interpretive mode, where we are given oral or visual input that we interpret according to our background knowledge, experiences, and emotions. It can be very personal. It is also what I call the "power mode." This is the mode where our learning journey begins. How we interpret the world outside of us begins with the world we know is inside of us. It is the catalyst and the context for the other modes of communication that we use. The second mode is the interpersonal mode, in which we share this information with others, having interpreted and run it through our personal filter. Finally, there's the mode of communication we use least often, and yet is the most commonly used in the classroom: the presentational mode, which is a one-way communication of information via oral or written "report." It is also the mode most used by the teacher, sometimes known as "sit and get" or "sage on the stage."

Because I was a language teacher, I had asked these same questions of my students, but I gave them multiple prompts and paths to expand and personalize their answers. Asking these questions wasn't an assessment; it was about communication — forging connections to build relationships with others and ourselves. The questions were meant for reflection and to help the child find his or her place in the world.

These three somewhat simple questions ultimately triggered a deeper frustration in me about what teaching had come to be. They reminded me of the ineffective and harmful ways we evaluate learning in school. Learning must be quantifiable and easy to put in a spreadsheet, to create statistics and data. In this age of computers and information exchange, communication has been reduced to a graphic, emoji, text-speak, selfie or data that can be easily given and then "digested." Bite-sized chunks. Easily shared via computers on the internet and through social media.

I know that this is the same frustration that teachers, students and parents are going through today with standardized testing and the prescribed paths to get there. There is so much more to life than that! Life doesn't come down to a test, we tell ourselves and our children, YET, we are not living this truth. Teachers and students are reduced to numbers. Learning experiences homogenized, pasteurized, and squeezed into a box for convenient consumption and control. Where is the meaning? What does it have to do with me, my life, and the real world? These are common questions that echo through the hallways in schools. If we are not curious and don't look inside to find the deeper meaning to our experiences and journey in life, then there is no awareness, learning, growth or perceived purpose to our path.

Yes, life is full of choices, multiple ones. Sometimes it is a 50/50 chance of being right, but we never know until more questions come up and we find ourselves with more choices to make. And more often than not, there are no right or wrong answers to the questions that do come up. We just have our perceptions, actions, and the lesson we are meant to learn from them that will lead us to the next step... and the next and the next. Life is about reflection and figuring out the next step. It is about a growth mindset of "not yet," but even more, it is about evolution and being and doing a little bit better today than we did yesterday or the day before or the day before that. So, put down the red pen and stop marking up your life with checkmarks, Xs and boxes. Instead, go inside and open your heart to the endless possibilities for your journey and your path in life. That is where true enlightenment and learning take place!

1

Lessons learned

1.1 Personal Reflection Activity

Answer the following questions about yourself.

    1. What is your name?

    2. Where are you from?

    3. What is your purpose?

1.2 Interpersonal Connection Activity

Ask someone you know and love what they believe their purpose in life is. Then, ask them to explain why they believe what they believe. Take notes for future use.

2

PIVOTAL MOMENTS

"The pivotal moments in your life are always made up of smaller pieces, things that seemed insignificant at time, but in fact brought you to where you needed to be."

— **ELIZABETH NORRIS,** *UNDONE*

AFFIRMATION:

*I am exactly where I need to be in order to learn
exactly what I am supposed to learn.*

So how did I end up embarking on the pilgrim's route to Santiago de Compostela at 60 years old, seeking answers to life's big questions? I had studied there fifteen years earlier at the University of Santiago de Compostela, something that marked a life-changing event in my life. It was the first time I had traveled without my family and experienced a solitary, nun-like life. There had been no TV, radio or other distractions that I could use as a means of escape. I had a cell phone, but it was too expensive to use it to call home and talk to family. So, I had my first glimpse into the power of silence and solitude that would open the window to a view of my inner self. I spent my time studying, reading books, and journaling.

To prepare for the trip, in a typical "teacher-like" fashion, I did a great deal of research, gathering together as much information as I could find on everything related to Santiago and the Spanish culture—particularly Galicia, the region in which Santiago is found. Perhaps to the surprise of some, it is quite different from the rest of Spain. First of all, the people there speak "gallego," which is a language heavily influenced from Portuguese, since it is not far from the border with Portugal. Climate-wise, it rains a lot and is cooler in temperature than the rest of Spain. Its geography looks much like the rolling green hills of Ireland, which may have been a factor in why Celtic tribes came to this region to settle. As a result, there is significant Celtic influence in their culture. They play an instrument similar to the bagpipes called the "gaeta," and dance the "jig" instead of flamenco. Many Celtic symbols can be seen in their cultural "products," such as monuments, buildings, jewelry, and pottery.

The influence of the Celts is also reflected in the practices and perspectives of the Galicians. They have a strong belief in the magic and mystery of nature. They also have a strong belief in fairies and the transmigration of souls, which connected to a book I'd brought along to read, in order to learn more about this region of Spain, *The Camino: A Journey of Spirit* by Shirley MacLaine. I knew nothing about it except that its title touched on something that came up repeatedly during my research about Santiago. The book is about Shirley MacLaine's journey on the Camino de Santiago as a pilgrim on a "brave personal quest seeking spiritual understanding."

More than anything else I'd discovered in my research, *this* resonated with me. I had learned just a little about the Camino in my college classes, but only to make connections as to how it was referenced in literature or history. The Camino, also known as the Way of St. James, is a network of pilgrims' ways that lead to the shrine of the apostle Saint James the Great in the cathedral of Santiago de Compostela, which is found in Galicia in northwestern Spain.

So why do pilgrims, or "peregrinos," go to Santiago? Legend

has it that the Apostle James was beheaded in Jerusalem in 44 A.D., where his head remained, but it is said that his body was brought by boat to Spain and buried in the "Campus Stellae," or "field of stars," which became known as Compostela. His remains were then discovered by a peasant shepherd named Pelayo in 812 A.D. and soon thereafter, many Christians throughout Europe began making religious pilgrimages there. In the 11th century, the construction of a magnificent cathedral was begun to house the remains of St. James, or "Sant Jacobo." There are many routes of the Camino, originating in various places throughout Europe. The most popular is the French Way, or the "Camino Francés," which originates in Saint Jean Pied-de-Port in the foothills of the Pyrenees mountains in France, and continues through the northern part of Spain for over 500 miles, eventually ending at the cathedral in Santiago de Compostela.

As I read Shirley MacLaine's book fifteen years earlier, I became more and more curious about my own spiritual journey and how things were manifesting in both my personal and professional life. Learning about the personal experiences and journeys of others can have that kind of power. My father had passed away a few years before, and since then, the dynamics within my birth family had become increasingly more difficult. I had also begun working at a school that had very high expectations and challenged me on every level of my being: energetically, mentally, physically and emotionally. So, in my silence and solitude, amid my traditional study at the university, I explored these aspects of my life, asking the same big questions: *Who am I?* and *What is my purpose?*

Amazingly enough, the questions I was asking inside then manifested outside. Everywhere I went in Santiago, from my classes to the city, I met people from all over the world, and had the chance to ask them those very questions. I gained so many new perspectives about being and purpose, especially from the pilgrims who had made the journey on the Camino, and had arrived in Santiago "a new person"—an enlightened person with a new, more awakened perspective on life. The stories of their struggles, their triumphs, and their discoveries were powerful, and left an impression on me. I knew in my heart that I would return to Santiago someday as a pilgrim.

2

Lessons learned

2.1 Personal Reflection Activity

True or false?

     1. Gaeta is a type of dance.

     2. Santiago means "St. James."

     3. People in Galicia speak Gaelic.

2.2 Interpersonal Connection Activity

During a meal with a friend or loved one, tell them what you have learned about Santiago de Compostela and the Camino so far. Ask them to tell you something about an experience they might have had when traveling and what they learned about the people, places, and things there.

3

VALIDATION

"I've talked to nearly 30,000 people on this show, and all 30,000 had one thing in common: They all wanted validation... I would tell you that every single person you will ever meet shares that common desire."

— OPRAH WINFREY
FINAL EPISODE OF "THE OPRAH WINFREY SHOW"

AFFIRMATION:

I do not need validation from others to know the truth and to be the authentic self that already lives inside me.

Back at the Pilgrim's Office, it was finally my turn! I walked up to the person behind the counter who immediately started asking me those three predictable questions. I tried to engage them in a deeper conversation, in Spanish no less, but he would have nothing of it.

"What is your name?" he asked. Question 1.

"Linda. What is your name?"

No answer. "Where are you from?" he asked. Question 2.

"I am from the United States. Florida, near Cape Canaveral, you know, where the rockets go off."

He cut me off. Time for Question 3. "What was the purpose of your camino, religious or spiritual?"

"Spiritual, actually. I learned so much about myself and met so many great people from all over the world. It was quite a life-changing experience that…"

He cut me off again, handing me a certificate in Latin called a compostela that basically said that I'd completed the requirements of the Camino. With this compostela, I was officially a "peregrina." A Pilgrim of the Camino. Then, with the wave of a hand and a "buen camino," he pointed to the exit door and motioned for me to leave.

Needless to say, I was disappointed by the experience in the Pilgrim's Office, with its formal summative assessment of me. But, the disappointment faded back into the elation I felt at my accomplishment. I was still floating on the energy of what I had experienced and learned on my journey along the way on the Camino, and that was enough. I was enough!

As I left the Pilgrim's Office with my compostela in hand, I ran into the Canadian sisters I had come to know along the Camino. They had arrived much earlier in Santiago, and were now on their way to the Pilgrim's Mass. I was greeted with Joan's harsh welcome. "You FINALLY made it!"

Susan trailed after, with a smile. "It is so good to see you."

Joan noted the compostela in my hand and chuckled. "Man, after all that walking, and all we get is a piece of paper. It's just like a certificate that we could easily create and print out on our own computer back home." Her diminishment reminded me of the Peanuts Halloween special, when Charlie Brown goes for "tricks and treats." Everyone else got a bunch of candy in their bags, but "all I got was a rock."

Susan stayed silent while Joan kept talking. She complained

that there was not more fanfare. She said that when they walked into the Plaza de Obradoiro in front of the majestic cathedral, she expected someone to be there to greet the pilgrims and congratulate them on their great accomplishment, like something we would see in an awards ceremony or at the finish line of an athletic event. It was clear she had not bothered to learn anything about the rituals or the symbolism in the cathedral, or the history and meaning behind the Camino, so her experience seemed somewhat superficial, without meaningful connections.

I considered Joan's reactions for a moment and felt a flood of questions. Are we just going through life with a checklist and a red pen? Is the goal to check things off our list so that we feel more accomplished and better about ourselves? Are we just pursuing a bucket list of experiences that have been marketed to us through commercials, advertisements, and pre-packaged tours of life? Are we gathering "Kodak" moments to share and post on social media so that others can envy us and wish their lives were more like ours? Are we just knocking on the doors of opportunity looking for either tricks or treats, and when it isn't what we expect, we think we just "got a rock?" Then, do we take that rock and put it in our knapsack and carry it with us until we reach the next door? OR, do we let it go, like some of the peregrinos on the Camino? Do we let it go, or do we stay weighed down, burdened, held back, and frozen?

When Susan got a moment to speak, she shared that she felt like she had learned so much on the Camino, about Spain and about herself. "This was a fantastic experience that I'll never forget," she gushed. She explained how she had made so many connections and grown so much as a person, in her knowledge of herself, her relationships and how she was so very grateful for the experience.

Hmm. I reflected on the sisters' opposing perspectives as I walked back to the hotel, feeling a lightness in each step I took. Their reactions were very familiar, and they exemplified something that I had witnessed in my career in the education system. Some educators, some students, some learners only have their eyes on the goal, the prize, the end "number," or the score. They fixate on how these results will bring recognition, reward, goals achieved and fulfillment of a list of expectations—even if they are not our own.

Others, however, are more focused on the journey, and how they are seeking growth to model for others. They aim to help nurture and grow experiences for children that will shape them into kind and loving human beings that will shine brightly and share their special gifts with the world. For some, the learning is in the head and stays there, where the Ego lies (the double meaning fully intended here). But for others, learning is about what touches the heart and what makes it grow, blossom, and sow seeds of hope for peace, love and joy for all of us! There is no doubt that for every human being, the journey between the head and the heart is where the greatest learning gains are made. That is what makes us human and sets us apart from other living creatures.

3

Lessons learned

3.1 Personal Reflection Activity

Answer the following questions.

    1. What is a compostela?

    2. What is a peregrina?

    3. What is done to recognize and celebrate a "true peregrina?"

3.2 Interpersonal Connection Activity

Talk to a friend or loved one and ask them to tell you about a time they accomplished, earned, or won something and how they felt. Take note of the details and words they use to describe it. How much of what they describe is data, goals, or "bucket list" achievements and how much of what they describe is about what they learned and the emotional experience they had?

4

CONTEXT AND LENSES

"For me context is the key – from that comes the understanding of everything."

— **KENNETH NOLAND, AMERICAN PAINTER**

AFFIRMATION:

I can look ahead of me, and I can look behind me, but most importantly, I must get curious and look within for clues that will guide me and lead me to the answers I am seeking.

Context is so important in life. Context is the best way to explain my journey before the journey: what led me to the start of my Camino. Context. Definition: "the circumstances that form the setting for an event, statement, or idea, and in terms of which it can be fully understood and assessed." It is critical to our learning path. Things taken out of context are misleading and can be misunderstood. Context gives meaning.

In education, greater connections are made and deeper learning occurs when we first build a foundation of background knowledge for the learner, and place it into a meaningful context for making connections. So, stay with me here on my learning journey, as we travel back and build some context that will help more clearly enlighten the path of my journey on the Camino. We don't need to dwell there. We must live in the present, as so many great teachers say, but it doesn't hurt to awaken and connect the dots to how we got to the present, so that we can learn and keep moving forward.

So, the context of my beginning: 1955, Ithaca, New York. Mother and father, a sister seven years older than me. My dad had his own business and was building a house on a hill when suddenly Hurricane Hazel came through and wiped out his business. He lost everything and had to declare bankruptcy. He wanted a new beginning, a new context. So he packed up the family and moved to Florida when I was still very young. I basically grew up in Florida near the beach. My family continued to struggle financially. My two younger brothers were born about 18 months apart. Around the same time, my sister got a staph infection in her leg from a mosquito bite and nearly died. She spent months in isolation recovering from surgery, first in a wheelchair and then on crutches.

Needless to say, my parents were overtaxed both physically and financially. I spent a lot of time with my maternal grandparents when my parents were at the hospital. When they were home, I spent my time helping my mom care for my younger brothers, disinfecting the house of the staph infection (today, called MRSA) and taking on adult-like responsibilities to care for others. I also lived in fear of getting the infection myself; I had to bathe daily in an awful smelling purple liquid as well as have huge boils that came up on my body lanced and drained.

The context of my early, formative years created a caretaker, a helper, a "good girl" who doesn't make demands on others. For survival in my volatile environment, I developed and nurtured "antennae" that would pick up the energy and signals of everyone and everything around me. I became an expert in personalizing and making connections to all my interactions and interpretations. It is what we do as human beings. Just look at Maslow's Hierarchy of Needs. I was operating in a context of the very lowest levels, physiological needs and safety needs. My basic survival needs of air, water, food and shelter were barely being met. As far as financial needs, personal safety, and health and well being, those were a constant challenge and most of the time, not met.

As a result, I kind of got stuck there, like many human beings. There were so many challenges and roadblocks to moving to the next level of human needs, which encompasses interpersonal relationships and feelings of acceptance and belonging. According to the research of Brené Brown, in the absence of love and belonging and joy, there is suffering. What I wanted more than anything was to be loved, to be happy, and to feel like I belonged to my family. Instead, I was isolated and left out most of the time because my needs were not as great as those of my siblings. I didn't want to be any more of a burden on my mom, so I stayed small and invisible.

Because I was so desperately needed at home, I didn't go to kindergarten. It wasn't required back then. So, it wasn't until I turned six that I entered first grade. My classmates had already attended a year of kindergarten and had a chance to experience some social-emotional learning. Nonetheless, many children, like me, come to school stuck in the lowest level of Maslow's Hierarchy. For some, basic needs of food, shelter and safety are not even being met. I know a teacher who goes to secondhand stores and buys clothes and shoes for students who she notices are wearing ragged ones, or who have come to school in dirty clothes that they turn inside out so that others won't notice that they're wearing the same clothes a second day in a row. I know a teacher who worked to get glasses for a student who squinted so badly in class to see the board, his eyes were beginning to cross. Yet, after he got the glasses, his mother took them and sold them for drug money. I know a teacher who has a basket in her room for children to put any uneaten food from their lunch trays so that she can make a care package to send home with certain students over the weekend so that they will have something to eat. I know a teacher who took a student into her home once she found out the girl was living in her car in a grocery store parking lot because she was too afraid to go home and be beaten and molested again.

For me, like for many children with unmet needs, school became a sanctuary, a place where I could escape the turmoil and sadness at home. It also became a source of activities that piqued my curiosity and sense of adventure. It was exciting and invigorating. I could explore knowledge, ask questions, and "escape" to a happier place, especially through books. My first grade teacher was like Miss Honey in *Matilda*. I felt safe and inspired to learn. I felt like I belonged there and that I was seen and heard and that I mattered. AND, I figured out quickly that the more I learned, the better grades I got. AND, the better grades I got, the more attention I got. AND, the more attention I got, the more I felt a sense of belonging, love and acceptance. I found a way to meet my own needs, and move up Maslow's Hierarchy.

From the day we are born until the day we die, the path that we follow is completely directed by the context of our lives and our interpretation of it. The events and people we encounter, both good and bad, shape the vision of ourselves and how we see the world. Our interpretation gives meaning to the circumstances and shapes our perception, or story, that we create about the circumstances, in order to help us to understand and make choices.

When I became a teacher myself, I used to tell my students that learning in my class was about getting new "lentes" (Spanish for "lenses") through which to see themselves and the world in which they lived. This is true for all of us. The "lentes" we wear as a result of our experiences become the filter for all input, and our interpretation of that input. It shapes our perspective, and subsequent values, beliefs, thoughts, choices, and actions. Each step we take in life is, therefore, taken from that perspective alone—unless we become aware of other perspectives, and make different choices based on those different perspectives.

In the world of languages, a culture is defined by the "three Ps"—products, practices, and perspectives. From human culture to the culture of a single person, everyone is defined by the things that surround them (products), their choices, actions and behaviors (practices), and the way they see the products and practices, plus the personal value they place on them (perspective).

To me, these "three Ps" are much more essential to learn about than the "three Rs" stereotypically touted in learning. Moreover, the three Ps are critical for learning in *life*, not just school. Nurture and develop the child within, and help them find their place in the context of the world outside of them. Developing and focusing our "lentes" for a greater, broader perspective helps us to see our place in the world, and this humanity is what we should be teaching. These "lentes," I used to tell my students, were the greatest "gift" they would receive on their learning journeys in my class.

As teachers, we need to understand that the children who come to our classroom every day share a similar human journey to ours, but may just be wearing different "lentes" to look at what we are showing and teaching them. Their learning journey starts with their personal context, and the way they interpret the world around them. So, how do we hook them, getting them to connect to us, and what we want them to learn?

This is the MOST essential of "Essential Questions." In education lingo, "Essential Questions" are deeper, more thought-provoking questions that drive lesson plans. Yet, somehow, this essence has become lost in an overstuffed, one-size-fits-all "bag of tricks" of prescribed best practices.

My experience has taught me that we must first connect with the content and our students through the human heart. It is from that place that we feel empathy and can make better choices. It is from there that we can be the best teachers we can possibly be, because our lesson plan is based on connection, and our essential questions are placed in a context of greater humanity. Our students are us, and we are our students. We are part of the human family. That which is in you is also in me. Learning becomes more relational than transactional. The teacher-student interaction is more like two hearts acting as a Venn Diagram rather than an exchange or delivery of "goods." Knowledge is not a commodity.

So, why don't we operate from there, instead of from external standards, prescribed lesson plans, checklists, and boxes, and everything impersonal? We are mechanizing the learning process as if we are living in the Industrial Age. Everything is about efficient production and tangible results. Teachers, students, and parents are just cogs in the wheels that are needed to move things "forward" and make progress. But what does that even mean? Where is the human context? How can that be personalized, and how can that create meaning that will motivate us to own our teaching and learning, when we are in front of a classroom of 20 to 30 young people, all with different contexts, perspectives, and learning needs?

We cannot develop a school culture of meaningful learning without first understanding what is within it—its products, practices, and perspectives—and how the culture fits into the larger context of humanity. Our own personal learning journey through life, outside of school, is the same. Real education, real growth, is about enlightenment, not measurement. Personal perspectives. Personal stories. Personal connections to human contexts and finding our place in the world. A journey of the human spirit.

We are all on this journey called life, but we are not all taking the same path. Yes, our paths will intersect, intertwine, merge, and diverge. There will be mountains and valleys, peaks and crevices.

Sometimes our path will be straight and clear, and sometimes it will be winding or muddy or foggy or rocky. We will be called to weather all possible conditions of the path on our journey. But the thing we need to remember is that it is our personal journey, we are never alone and as long as we figure out how to keep putting one foot in front of the other, we will reach our destination. We will meet people along the way. Some will stay with us and will help support and guide us, and sometimes we will be called to be the support and guidance for others.

As human beings, we are both teachers and learners. That is our journey. We are not born perfect. We are not born knowing everything. We are born to grow, learn, and develop into the best versions of ourselves that we possibly can be. Each day is an opportunity to become better than who we were yesterday. Those are true learning gains, but how can we measure that in the current educational system of standardization and continuous feedback of "not enough?" How do we assess the learning at the end of a journey more holistically, instead of three oversimplified multiple choice questions? Everyone seems so discontent with the way of the world today… with overwhelming feelings of anxiety, stress, anger and frustration. Of never being able to have enough, or do enough, or be enough.

How do we change this? It starts within each of us and then, it's passed on to others, especially children. The world can be changed one child at a time—for good or for bad—and we each need to ask ourselves what role we will play in that change. What difference will we make in the world or what indifference will make and define us and the part we play in this world?

4

Lessons learned

4.1 Personal Reflection Activity

Complete the following chart. How are we alike? How are we different? Share a life lesson you learned from your context.

	Linda's context	*My context*
Year born		
Place born		
Number of siblings		
Positive childhood emotions		
Negative childhood emotions		

Lessons learned:

4.2 Interpersonal Connection Activity

Think of a friend or loved one that you would like to know more about their "context". Send them an email or a hand-written letter and ask them to tell you about a lesson they learned in life and how their circumstances/context affected that.

5

MAKING A DIFFERENCE

"When I ask teachers why they teach, they almost always say that it is because they want to make a difference in the lives of children."

— ARNE DUNCAN
U.S. SECRETARY OF EDUCATION (2009-2015)

AFFIRMATION:

I make a difference in my life and in the lives of others every time I make a choice.

Once I began school, my teachers became my role models and my source of inspiration and affirmation. As long as I got good grades and excellent behavior marks, I felt good about myself. I continued on this path during my elementary, junior high, high school, and college years.

The one time I was told I was not "good enough," was when I entered my Spanish II class in 9th grade. I had taken Spanish I in junior high. My teacher was not a Spanish teacher, but rather, a history teacher who didn't speak Spanish. We listened to dialogues on tapes, memorized the dialogues, and recited them in front of the class. If we sounded anything like the voice on the tape, the teacher gave us an A, and we "passed" the class. Pure memorization and regurgitation...the old school gold standard of learning and education.

When we all got to the high school, we were placed in Spanish II, in Señorita Ortiz's class. Señorita Ortiz was only about 4'10" tall, but in the minds of her students and colleagues, she was larger than life. She was a force to be reckoned with! She was a native speaker from Spain, *una castellana* from the very center of the Spanish language and cultural identity, no less. She told us all on the first day of class that we had not learned enough to be in her class and that we had to all go back to Spanish I. Well, my 14-year-old self was outraged and indignant! *What?* How could this be? I had done everything that was asked of me. I had memorized all of those dialogues and recited them perfectly. I had already been affirmed with an A. (Is that what "A" stands for in our grading system? A for Affirmed, B means you can do Better, C means you Can't, D for Dumb, and F for Failure… all disguised as letters of the dear alphabet we so lovingly learn and recite from the first day of learning in school? A trick, like the "piggyback" songs we sang that were disguised to try to help us learn and remember knowledge better? Like how the tune of "Twinkle Twinkle Little Star" was repurposed as the Alphabet Song?)

I went to Señorita Ortiz and TOLD her that I had done everything that was required of me, and that I WAS NOT GOING BACK to Spanish I. I was NOT a FAILURE! (Again: 14 years old.)

She looked at me, and gently asked a grammar question. "What is the difference between SER and ESTAR?"

Well, my mind quickly went to lines in the memorized dialogues, where there were similar versions of these words like "¿cómo estás? or "quiero ser mecánico." I proudly recited those lines from the dialogues to her, looking into her eyes for approval and affirmation.

She just shook her head and said, "No. What are the rules for when to use them?"

RULES? I hadn't learned any rules about them, so I told her that, to which she replied, "That's exactly why you need to go back to Spanish I. You didn't learn what you were supposed to learn to be able to do Spanish II."

There it was… no validation here, which is why a flood of emotions like shame, disappointment, anger and frustration came bursting forth like a herd of bulls during San Fermín in Pamplona. WHY didn't that teacher in 8th grade teach me what I needed to know? WHY did another adult let me down? WHY was this new teacher telling me I was "not enough?"

Then, everything changed. Sensing these emotions in me, Señorita Ortiz spoke up again. "You want to go on to Spanish II? I'll tell you what. I believe in you, and believe you have potential. You come EVERY DAY after school for one hour, and I will teach you what you didn't learn in Spanish I. You have until the end of the first grading period to catch up and learn what you need to know. If you don't, you will go back to Spanish I. Deal?"

Whoa…what was that? Validation? Hope? *She believes in me? I have potential? I have a choice?* I was given the power to choose, and I did. I went every day after school and eagerly learned what she had to teach me. Her belief in me and the way she empowered me with my own personal choice to learn completely changed my feelings toward the subject matter, as well as how I felt about myself. The loving lesson she taught me through her empathy, kindness and generosity in that moment was greater than any grammar lesson I learned from her about the verbs SER and ESTAR. I became inspired to learn more languages, taking on French in 10th grade and German in 11th. I went on to major in languages in college and eventually, became a language teacher myself.

But Señorita Ortiz was not the only teacher to have an impact on my life and how I saw myself in the world. Her loving kindness and gift of another chance sprinkled with hope and belief transformed my world inside forever. She modeled patience, compassion, the power of "not yet" and "sí, se puede" (yes, you can!). I would carry these values with me into my own classroom.

That is the power of teaching. With each teacher we have, there are life lessons that help lead us to learn just a little more about ourselves and our journey in life. It's not just about the italicized or emboldened words in a textbook or the checklist of criteria called standards that show up on a standardized and limiting discrete item test. It's about deep, meaningful and personal learning! The personal learning experiences that I had as a result of my own teachers touched my heart.

There was Mr. Allen, who looked like Fred Flintstone and wore tennis shoes with a suit everyday. He was my high school English and Humanities teacher. Mr. Allen showed me a world of possibilities to explore and be curious about. How the three Ps of humanity—products, practices, and perspectives—played out in what we wrote down in words and illustrations. He opened my mind and heart to the power of the arts to inspire creativity and hope. He left the "bread crumbs and fairy dust" for me to make connections for myself with all of history and all people. He helped me find my place among many in the world. His passion for the subject matter was so intense that you couldn't help but get hooked and love it too.

Years later, I made the connection that you can anagram the word PASSION to I PASS ON. This transformed the way I thought about passion, and the way it can become legacy. Mr. Allen passed on his passion for the humanities and the human connection to me, and I hope I've passed it on to my own students.

There was Dr. Pérez, my college Spanish teacher who was from Cuba and had chosen to leave her country and most of her family because of the political climate of the time. She shared her story of feeling disconnected from her identity as she tried to establish new connections to herself and family in the United

States. Yet, there was still a core part of her that connected to her identity and home in Cuba. To get to know her culture and her "people" better, she invited students to her house for a typical Cuban meal and conversation, to experience a real context and meaning behind why we were learning Spanish. I cherish those memories, and the gift she gave us with her generosity.

There was Dr. Godoy, also a college professor from Cuba, who wore a suit and bow tie to class every day. He too shared stories of his personal struggle to assimilate into a new culture and identity. He had been teaching at a university in Cuba, but he and his family arrived in the U.S. with only the clothes on their backs. His doctorate degree from Cuba was not recognized as valid to teach in an American university, so he had to work as a janitor in a local high school in Miami, and go back to school at night to get another doctorate degree to be able to teach at the university there. He could barely speak English or make ends meet, and he had to dig through dumpsters behind the grocery store for food to feed his family. He was an educated, sophisticated, proud man who taught me about being human, humble, and vulnerable. Looking back now, some 40 years later, I realize that he, like many other teachers, also taught me about staying connected to who you are and who you want to be, and to stay focused on manifesting that in your life every day.

There was Madame Carrell, my French college professor who was very demanding and believed I could accomplish whatever I set my mind to do. I learned lessons from her about persistence, perseverance, and personalization of learning. I'd only had two years of high school French, and yet, she saw potential in my language skills and placed me in not one, but TWO 300-level French literature courses. She was also my advisor, whom I BEGGED to be placed in another course, because I was wearing out my dictionary, patience, self-esteem and tear ducts.

Madame Carrell could see I was struggling, so she introduced me to another young woman in the class who had been in my position the previous semester, and suggested we study together. She also asked me to stay after every class to make sure I had understood the lecture and taken appropriate notes to prepare for the test. I even noticed that her lectures changed in order to accommodate a more structured and patterned approach to the material, making it easier to "digest" and learn for the test. Structure notwithstanding, the content she presented about French authors and their works was personalized, connected to our lives and not just a slew of facts and dates. She helped us to understand how the book we were reading (in French, no less) was a story that reflected the perspective of the author's personal life, their historical context, and artistic contributions to the world. Their stories were our stories... very human, personal, and real.

Of course, there are also great teachers, whose influence I have felt profoundly, that the entire world has access to today. Miguel de Cervantes's novel and protagonist, *Don Quixote*, imparted lessons of idealism and the good of people. Jaime Escalante, the real-life math teacher portrayed in the 1988 film *Stand and Deliver* gave me "ganas." A bit difficult to translate into English, "ganas" is an unstoppable desire to learn and succeed, no matter the obstacles or limiting labels. Mr. Escalante also believed that students would "rise to the level of expectation," and I embraced the same belief in my own classroom.

Even though I was already an adult when *Mister Rogers' Neighborhood* first aired, I still consider Fred Rogers one of my greatest teachers. Mister Rogers told children and adults alike: "You are special, and I love you just the way you are." He taught inclusion, acceptance, and being a good "neighbor" through unconditional love and empathy. His episodes showed that learning is about curiosity and adventure, as we traveled every episode to the Land of Make-Believe and got to explore.

Maya Angelou modeled that you can overcome anything,

sing your song, share your unique gifts with the world, and be the rainbow in someone else's cloud. When I first read *I Know Why the Caged Bird Sings*, I was a high school senior, wanting to go to college, break free from my family, and discover my heartfelt place in the world. Reading that book let me know there was a song inside of me, and that I had to share it with the world. This is one of the most significant lessons we'll ever learn, and one that teachers embody wholly. The best teachers set us on our greatest journey: the one that lights the way back to our True Self.

5

Lessons learned

5.1 Personal Reflection Activity

Write a letter to a teacher who made a difference in your life. Be sure to thank them and explain how they impacted your life. Find a way to mail the letter or send the email to that teacher and see what their response is to how YOU may have had a lasting impact on their life and career.

5.2 Interpersonal Connection Activity

Where do you fit into the bigger picture of the world? Think about 5 things you can do daily that will have a positive impact on others and the world around you. Complete the drawing below by either drawing or cutting out pictures or using computer graphics to illustrate your intended thoughts and actions.

6

STEPPING STONES ON THE
LEARNING PATH

*"No one is dumb who is curious. The people who don't
ask questions remain clueless throughout their lives."*

— NEIL DEGRASSE TYSON, ASTROPHYSICIST

AFFIRMATION:

*I always seek to learn and grow into a better
version of myself today than existed yesterday.*

I arrived at the Orlando airport around 5:00 pm for my flight
to Madrid. Fortunately, it was a direct flight; I landed at the
Madrid-Barajas Airport around 9:00 am the next morning, after
a sleepless night in a cramped seat. Instead of resting, I spent
the time worrying that my backpack would somehow get lost or
stolen. My overstuffed overweight backpack: my survival source,
full of everything that I needed. If I didn't have that, I wouldn't
have what I needed to do the Camino. I'd be forced to return
home with an unfulfilled dream.

When I was a teacher, I always safeguarded my lessons and
teaching materials like they were the treasure to my soul. I shared
them graciously and generously with my students, but I guarded
and kept them secret from colleagues because of fear. I was afraid
of judgment. I was afraid of criticism. I was afraid of ridicule.

The first time I gave a professional development session, I co-presented with a colleague on the new standards that were about to be implemented for the first time ever. She and I had served on the state and district committees for writing these standards, and so we were asked to present them to other teachers. She and I opened up our "bag of tricks" and shared everything we had created. I don't remember much about what we presented, but I remembered the way I felt after presenting them.

During the presentation, some teachers were grading papers. Some were talking in the back of the room. Some were on their cell phones. Some were asking questions, and trying to write down everything we said. Some were taking notes all over the handouts. Some seemed excited, but most seemed disengaged, distracted, and disinterested.

I felt confused. The students loved these activities, and we had great results with them in the classroom. What was going on with the teachers? My colleague and I had spent hours and hours preparing this presentation, only to put ourselves out there and feel the humiliation of rejection. Yikes! How could these teachers be so ungrateful and rude? I would not have accepted this kind of behavior in the classroom, but in truth, I'd never really experienced it with students. There were a few students each year who were armored up, and closed off to what I was trying to "share" with them, but nothing like this, and not on such a grand scale.

Some teachers left at lunchtime and didn't return. Some were late coming back from lunch and had a difficult time staying awake, but we pushed on until the end of the seven hour training. After we finished, a couple of teachers stayed after to ask questions, but what really shocked me was that two teachers stayed and waited just to tell us this: "You must not have a life outside of school. This is A LOT of work, and we don't have the time to do all this nonsense. We just want you to know that we are never going to use any of this stuff, but thanks for sharing it anyway."

I will never forget how crushed I was by their comments. I stood there open-mouthed, shocked, as they left the room. As soon as the last person was gone, I burst into tears. My colleague was angered by their comments, but then had the enviable ability to just brush it off. She snorted with derision. "What do they know, anyway?"

I, not in possession of this enviable ability, was devastated. I took what they had said to heart. Others would probably tell me, as I have been told many times in my life, that I took it "personally." I have always been confused by that because if someone is saying something TO YOU and it is ABOUT YOU, then how can it not be personal?

Years later, on a journey that was beginning on this very flight to Madrid, I would realize that my interpretation was personalized, but only to my Ego, which is not my True Self. It was also personalized in that I chose to own what wasn't mine, only because my own personal experiences were being triggered. Context, "lentes," and perspective. For those teachers, their comments were personalized through the lens of their frustration and fear that they would not be enough. That they would not have enough time, enough resources, enough information or skills to implement the activities with their students, let alone be able to create more of their own to use in their classrooms. I felt like I hadn't been enough, and they felt like they couldn't be enough doing someone else's lesson plan.

•   •   •

During the long overseas flight, I noticed that the lady sitting next to me was wearing hiking-type clothes similar to mine. So, I struck up a conversation, using the typical questions that I had taught my Spanish students to ask when they converse with a "real live native speaker." It was a way of making a connection. The questions were the conduit between their hearts, I would tell them. "Who...?" "What...?" "Where..." "When...?" "Why...?" "How...?" The "WWWWWH" of communication. No matter if you are giving the information or receiving it, these are the important details. They also follow Bloom's Taxonomy of "higher order thinking," which means you are deepening your understanding, broadening your knowledge, and getting smarter, better informed, and empowered. Students always responded well to that idea!

"Hi! My name is Linda. What is your name?" Her name was Judy.

"Where are you from?" She was from Connecticut.

"Where are you going?" She was obviously going to Madrid, but from there, she was taking a train to St. Jean Pied de Port.

Ding-ding-ding! There was the REAL connection. "Oh my gosh! Are you walking the Camino?"

We then spent the next several hours talking about the "WWWWWH" of our stories. She had been a teacher too, and was an avid hiker. It turns out she had far more sophisticated equipment for hiking than I did, like a GPS watch. She also had a tent and a sleeping bag because she planned on sleeping in the wilderness. She and her family had done wilderness hiking and camping out west, so she spoke quite confidently of what she expected on the Camino and how she would handle it.

Fear began to take hold of me as I felt unprepared and uncertain of how I would handle everything. Fear had been a regular visitor during my Camino preparation process, but when I'd boarded the plane, the fear had quieted a bit, in lieu of my nervous excitement to start my journey, and my faith in my enormous backpack full of everything I needed. But now I was discovering that maybe I wasn't as prepared as I should be. I didn't have a sleeping bag nor a tent, but then, I was hoping to make it to my pre-arranged lodging each night.

But WHAT IF I didn't? What would I do? What would happen to me?

F-E-A-R—Feeling Every Added Regret!

I regretted not buying a sleeping bag and tent. I regretted not researching and buying a specialized hiking GPS fancy watch. Oh no, Dorothy! I would never get to the land of Oz!

Just as I was beginning to formulate an escape plan for when I arrived in Madrid, Judy said, "The one thing that makes me a little nervous is that I don't speak the language."

BAM! There it was, my salvation! I *did* speak the language, plus I knew a lot about those products, practices and perspectives of Spanish culture.

You've got this! my mind told me, more confident. But not for long. Judy asked where I was starting to walk.

"León," I replied, and explained why. León is located west of a grueling stretch of the Camino called the Meseta, which challenges hikers with its open sun exposure, vast flat landscapes, and dry heat. León is a little less than 200 miles from Santiago, and I had decided it wasn't important how many miles I did, so I opted to begin there and forgo the perils of the Meseta.

She followed up quickly. "Oh, well I'm going ALL the way. The whole 500 miles from St. Jean Pied de Port to Santiago. I may even go the rest of the way to Finisterra, on the coast. Not many people do that, you know."

My heart sank into my stomach again. I had wanted to start in St. Jean. I had wanted to do the whole 500 miles. I had even wanted to go to Finisterra, a storied place whose name literally means "land's end."

Finisterra fascinated me. Before Christopher Columbus's journey in 1492, this cape that juts out along the coast of Galicia was the farthest known point west on the European continent. The end of the known Earth that was feared by all, but where many pagan groups came to worship and perform rituals to the sun that set in the west, as if falling off the end of the Earth. To some, a land of death, and to others, a land of beginnings. There's a legend that Finisterra might be where the mythical city of Atlantis could be found, and a legend that St. James' head arrived near here, by boat, to be reunited with the body.

Suddenly it seemed like Finisterra was crucial to the journey I expected to have on the Camino. I wanted to be renewed, and experience a "new me" rising from the ashes like the Phoenix. Would that not happen if I didn't go to Finisterra? Not five minutes after wondering if I could put together an escape plan, I began to mentally calculate if I could continue on to the "land's end," and keep going after Santiago.

When we landed, I bid farewell to Judy, who went on her way to catch the train to St. Jean Pied to Port. Then I gathered my monstrous backpack, relieved that it safely chugged out onto the conveyor belt in baggage claim. It was the size and weight of a small child, so it took some maneuvering to wrestle it onto my back. I was too naive then, too attached to its contents, to realize that I had included everything in that backpack from fear. This burdensome weight was the sum total of my fear, from my childhood until today in Barajas Airport.

But I didn't know that yet. So with my "small child" in tow, I found my way to Chamartín Station where I boarded a train to León. This seems very mundane, but let me say: I love trains so much. I don't know what it is about them. Perhaps I was a conductor in another lifetime? I feel such peace when I am on a train. I love that they have more open space than an airplane, but most of all, I love the way trains travel through the countryside like a bird in flight through Mother Nature. There is a feeling of serenity and presence for me on a train, an almost dream-like feeling similar to the peaceful sensation I have when meditating.

It's fitting, perhaps, that when I settled into my train seat with the hope of getting a little sleep, I noticed a book on the floor near my feet. It was in Spanish, and I immediately recognized a familiar face on the cover. It was Deepak Chopra. I was already acquainted with Deepak's spiritual work, and had even participated in some of his meditation series. But there was truly no one's face I least expected to see on a stray book cover in Spain! *What? Deepak in Spain? Deepak in... Spanish?!* What was even more amazing was the title: "El camino hacia el amor: Como transformar nuestra vida colmándola de amor."

Translation is a tricky business. Translate, from Latin, literally means to "carry across" from one side to another. The power of words to bring meaning to any context in life is immeasurable. But if we translate everything literally, word-for-word, at face value, we lose meaning. If we translate using an online tool, there is still a danger of not accurately interpreting the intention or meaning behind the word and, therefore, we might use a completely incorrect word that paints a whole different picture than the message we intended.

Obviously, these pitfalls came up a lot in world language teaching. I used to share an example with my students to communicate the perils of direct translation. Parker Pen Company, a manufacturer of luxury pens, once had a marketing slogan in English that was: "It won't leak in your pocket and embarrass you." However, when the company translated the slogan to Spanish, they used the word "embarazar," as if it actually meant the word "embarrassed." In reality, "embarazar" means to impregnate or get pregnant! You can imagine the fiasco that ensued in Spanish-speaking markets.

The Spanish translation of Deepak's book is: "The Path to

Love: How to transform our life filling it to the brim with love." In English, however, I have seen many different versions: "The Path to Love: Renewing the Power of Spirit in Your Life." "Return to Love: Spiritual Strategies for Healing." "Return to Love: Spiritual Lessons for Creating the Love You Need." They each have a similar concept, but depending on the interpretation of the individual, could take on a whole new meaning. Since I am all about "spirit" and healing, I personally like the first one.

I picked up the book and opened it to a "random" page, which, of course, was not random at all. I was being shown the exact message I needed to read on the train whizzing toward León. That's a wonderful thought, isn't it? The Universe is always providing us with EXACTLY what we need in every moment, during every step.

Here's a loose translation of what I read that day, and exactly what I needed to calm my fears and help me take next step of my journey:

"When you truly find love, you find yourself. In the end, the journey is not a choice as we all must discover who we truly are. Such is our spiritual journey."

Love is the path. Love is the essential answer to life's essential questions. This lesson would be presented to me over and over again on the Camino. In truth, it had presented itself routinely since the day I was born, but I still needed to be reminded of it. I still needed the practice and experience in order to embody learning it. I will continue this lesson until the day I die!

Lulled by the peaceful rhythm of the train and Deepak's reassuring words, I slept the rest of the way to León.

6

Lessons learned

6.1 Personal Reflection Activity

Create a storyboard or comic strip of your dream life that includes details of "who," "what," "where," "when," "why," and "how" of your dream.

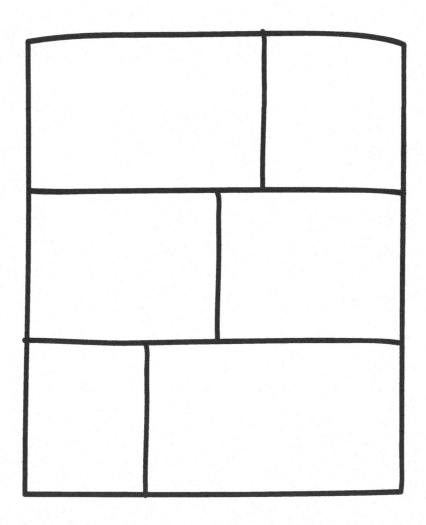

6.2 Interpersonal Connection Activity

Talk to an older family member and ask them what their dreams in life were and what happened in their life that either helped them realize their dreams or kept them from realizing their dreams.

Be sure to get more details by asking "who," "what," "where," "when," "why," and "how" questions followed by affirming statements/inquiries from the list below:

- I understand.

- Tell me more.

- Wow, that must have been hard (challenging, frustrating…)

- Wow, that must have been exciting (inspiring, fulfilling…)

- How did that make you feel?

- What did you learn from that experience?

- If you had to do it all over again, what would you change…what would you keep the same, and why or why not?

- What do you think would have happened if you had done "X" instead of "Y" instead?

7

F.A.I.L.: FAITHFUL ATTEMPTS IN LEARNING

"At the end of the day, when it comes time to make that decision, all you have to guide you are your values, and your vision and your life experiences that make you who you are."

— MICHELLE OBAMA, ATTORNEY, AUTHOR, FIRST LADY

AFFIRMATION:

I see myself and my place in the world through the lens of my soul.

When I became a teacher, it did not take long for me to realize that, in order to be a better and more effective teacher for my students, I needed to bring real life experiences into the classroom. Particularly as a world languages teacher, I needed to replicate situations that I had experienced in my own language learning, and provide meaningful contexts in which my students could interact and have more "authentic" experiences. This would engage their curiosity and encourage them to take adventures in learning that would challenge them to "figure it out." This is how we make true learning gains to keep moving forward and to grow more from each learning opportunity in life.

Sadly, I did not start there though. Like most teachers, I came out of college "armed" with an arsenal of textbook theories, methodologies, and curriculum that were considered the Best and Most Effective Way to Teach.

Of course, as any first-year teacher will tell you, those quickly fly out the window on the first day of class when you have late students, interruptions from the office, a fire drill or pep rally, equipment that doesn't work, or long lines at the copying machine. Or it's likely you got caught in traffic, spilled your coffee down the front of you, got your period, forgot your lunch, or suddenly encountered an angry parent at your classroom door. There are now a hundred plates spinning in the air, and your head is spinning out of control along with your emotions.

My older daughter also became a teacher, and at the end of her very first day in the classroom, I asked her what her first impression was. She used a great metaphor to describe her experience. She said, "Mom, it was like I was a firefighter and not a teacher. I felt like there were fires popping up all around me, and the minute I would put one out, another would flare up nearby. I would focus on putting that one out, then turn around and immediately see the other one I thought I'd put out was blazing again. By the end of the day, my only goal was not to put out all the fires, but to just keep from being engulfed in all the flames!"

When stress and "flames" kick in, it's natural to unconsciously switch into cruise control. We revert back to what is easiest and most comfortable. We teach the way we were taught and imitate the lessons we experienced as a student...the good, the bad and the ugly. It is thus that the cycle begins and cannot be broken until we make a conscious effort to change it. And to do that, we must raise our awareness and set our intentions of what we do want to manifest. This, I would discover, is a lifelong lesson plan—and not just for teachers.

My own first teaching job was in Brooklyn, New York. I taught Spanish, which I was certified in, and I also taught math and typing, which I wasn't certified in. I was good in math and had taken classes through calculus, so teaching algebra and geometry were not too challenging. I just had to do the assignment the night before I taught it to the students and make sure I understood it enough to answer their questions and get the "right final answer." I was in survival mode, and just cared about keeping one step ahead of humiliation and being "found out" that I wasn't certified to teach math (yet).

I was able to teach typing because my mom had made me take it in high school. She never thought I would attend college, since no one before me in my family had done so, and wanted me to have the skills needed to get a "decent job" as a secretary. I obediently followed her direction, and took typing and shorthand classes. But when I graduated, I bitterly wished I had instead taken more advanced classes, as they would have weighted my GPA the extra tenth of a point that ended up keeping me from being salutatorian of my class. I later realized that those classes were more valuable to me in life than the title of salutatorian: my first hint at what is truly essential in one's educational path and what is not.

Both passion and fear fueled my journey in that first year of teaching. I loved teaching and seeing the students learn, but it was a struggle as I tried to keep all those "plates spinning" in order to be successful. I was very concerned with failing—failing myself, failing the school administration, failing my students. It was an enormous amount of pressure, and many days felt like I was navigating a battlefield of landmines to avoid.

I don't remember what exactly I taught, in terms of curriculum, nor what the standards were. They didn't even exist back then. I do remember that I just took one step at a time and figured out how to get to the next step, the next page in the textbook, then the next chapter in the textbook. It was pure survival. I was living the experience of being a teacher. No more theory. I had choices to make daily about what I was going to do and how I was going to do it, but I didn't have an endless checklist of unrealistic expectations nor a prescription of cryptic strategies given to me by someone else. I followed the book, but I also followed my heart and took my cues from the students. How did they feel about how and what they were learning? I asked the students to reflect on those questions and then, I reflected on their answers. I wanted their experiences to be meaningful, positive and rewarding emotionally. I was instinctively following my heart to drive my teaching. Teaching really is a "work of heart."

Even though I don't remember all my teaching material, I am reminded that life is about human connections and relationships—especially in teaching. I do still remember many of my students from that first year, and how they made me feel successful, even when I was struggling and feeling like I failed. They made me feel loved, even though I was strict and had high expectations of them, because they knew that I was coming from a place of love and belief in their gifts. They made me feel hopeful because I had inspired them with my passion and excitement for learning and growing. I listened to their problems, both personal and academic, and tried to get to know them and their families better so that I could make the heart connections necessary for relationship building. I allowed my strengths of empathy, compassion, and loving kindness to drive my thoughts and actions. I relied on vulnerability to keep me balanced and on my path. I tried to look beyond any "flaws" in my students into the light of their potential and the possibilities of their path with the hope that they would reflect that back to me. And it worked well.

I lived in New York for two years, then returned to Florida, where I taught full-time for two years, before taking time off to have a baby. But even as a new mom, I missed teaching and being with students. It was as if there were a hole in my heart. So, I thought about what I had to offer the world, and tried to see my own "gifts" the way I did my students'. What could I do where I could be of service to others and share my gifts? There was an increasing Spanish-speaking population in our community and a great need for interpreters in the systems like the courts, human resources departments, law enforcement, health care.

So, I did some interpreting in court cases, at the police station, in the hospitals, but I felt that the people working in those positions needed to take greater efforts to connect with the Hispanic person they were working with. So, I offered classes in basic Spanish. Fill in the blank: "Basic Spanish for _____." Legal services, law enforcement, health care workers, etc. We just worked on basic phrases and the kinds of communication needed to make heart connections: "What is your name?" "What happened?" "What do you need?" "How can I help?" I taught them phrases to get to know the person better, but also that could be used to distract and calm them: "What is your favorite_____?" Another fill-in-the-blank: food, sport, actor, thing to do, etc. They also learned basic vocabulary words related to their individual context. Legal: "Do you have a lawyer?" Law enforcement: "Stop, put your hands up." Health care: "Where does it hurt?

It was personalized, manageable, and meaningful. The result was that everyone felt more empowered, empathic, and effective through these few phrases that opened the heart and made a connection. Did I know all the vocabulary? Not for all these specialized industries. But vocabulary wasn't really the point. Effective communication, like teaching, is about making a heart connection and being open to what is called "negotiation of meaning" in second language acquisition theory. This means asking questions, being curious, being in tune to body language, using circumlocution (describing something when you don't know the exact word)... all in an effort to figure out meaning. Real meaning exists beyond simple "comprehension."

7

Lessons learned

7.1 Personal Reflection Activity

Use these lenses to see 20 years into the future. Draw a picture of what you see.

7.2 Interpersonal Connection Activity

When you are out in your community, ask the people you meet if they know another language. If they do, find out how that has changed their perception of themselves and of the world around them as well as how they have benefitted from this skill. If they do not know another languages, ask them why not.

8

IMPOSTER SYNDROME

"I have written eleven books, but each time I think,
'Uh-oh, they're going to find me out now.'"

— MAYA ANGELOU, POET & AUTHOR

AFFIRMATION:

I am who I am and that is who I am meant to be,
always and forever, and that is enough.

I had arrived in León a couple of days prior to my planned start on the Camino. Ever the cautious yet curious traveler, I wanted to give myself time to adjust to the new time, and explore a little of León. I chose to stay at the "Casa de espiritualidad" at the Colegiata Isodoro. Located next to the Cathedral of León, it is part of an architectural complex that is, all at once, a temple, royal pantheon, convent, palace, library, and museum. The Royal Pantheon paintings are considered "the Sistine Chapel of the Romanic era." Everything there is beautifully inspiring. The rooms are in the cloistered part of the complex. How appropriate—a retreat to solitude, simplicity, and silence to contemplate all that is outside of us and discover all that is inside of us.

I decided to walk around and explore León. I wanted to find the Pilgrim's Credential Office and get my first official stamp in my Pilgrim's Passport, also known in Spanish as the "credencial." The credencial is a document that identifies you as a pilgrim and allows you to stay in albergues (special pilgrim hostels) at special rates, as well as to purchase a special "pilgrim's meal" provided in local bars and restaurants. The credencial is also a document that the pilgrim uses to authenticate his or her progress by obtaining sellos (stamps) along the way. Sellos can be acquired at most hotels and inns, restaurants, bars, churches, museums, city halls, police stations, and at all albergues. When the pilgrim reaches the Pilgrim's Office in Santiago, they can present the stamped credencial to confirm that they have walked at least the last 100 kilometers or cycled at least the last 200 kilometers, whereupon they are able to receive a Compostela, the document that certifies their pilgrimage.

As you may have gathered, there are countless places to get a stamp for one's credencial. Why did I think I needed to get a stamp from the Pilgrim's Credential Office in León? I knew I could get it from the hotel I was staying in, or at the Cathedral next door, or in the Museum across the street, or the restaurant around the corner. What was driving this need to be "validated" with a stamp for the "official" Pilgrim's Credential Office in León? Once again, I was looking for validation outside of me, something that I felt was more important, more empowering, more real. It tapped into that illusion of who I thought I was as a reflection of what I did. It tapped into those feelings of needing more, more, more because if I didn't have it, then I would be less, less, less.

But on another level, it tapped into a feeling of wanting and needing to be validated by the "official" and "authentic" place… something that I had always sought in life. To be real, true and authentic in who I am and what I do. What better way than confirmation by the ultimate authority? Authentic was always what I sought to be, but it was not always what I was able to manifest because of fear, Ego and feelings of "not enough."

What is really interesting is that the word "credential" derives from the Latin verb "credere," which means "to believe." So, this begs the question: are credentials, the validations we seek from others, based on who *they* believe we are, because of what we've accomplished, or do they derive from who *we* believe we truly are? This was a big question, and I was about to get multiple opportunities to reflect more, seek deeper understandings, and experience some real, meaningful lessons that would last me a lifetime.

Armed with a paper map and my phone GPS, I set out to find the preeminent Pilgrim's Credential Office for my authentic validation. As I got more and more lost and turned around, I stopped to ask locals for directions. I was given directions to go north, south, east and west. Turn right, left, straight ahead. After a couple of hours, I ended up in front of the Corte Inglés, a famous department store found throughout the bigger cities in Spain. This was very much not the Pilgrim's Credential Office.

As I gazed up at the massive commercial retail building filled with all kinds of material goods known to man, I noticed I was standing next to a large light pole. On that pole was a handmade sign that said "Diós me guía," "God guides me." *Hello again, Universe!* I had just spent two hours letting maps and other outside influences guide me instead of my own intuition and trust in myself. The truth was, I had betrayed myself over and over again, because of fear and lack of faith in myself, despite all the titles achieved, the awards and recognitions received or the long list of accomplishments I could fit on my resumé. I didn't trust myself, and this was the first opportunity in a series of many on the Camino to practice making a different choice.

With a chuckle, I put my maps away and abandoned my dogged quest for the Pilgrim's Credential Office. I instead returned to my accommodation, the Colegiata Isodoro, where I easily acquired the first stamps in my credencial. To this day, they are symbols of the first lessons I learned on the Camino, in a gentle nudge from the Universe to trust that I didn't need to project outside of myself for "enoughness." And to this day, I have never actually been to the Pilgrim's Credential Office in León.

• • •

That evening, I went to the Pilgrim's Mass in the León Cathedral. There were about 20-25 pilgrims there, mostly young people. My heart immediately opened up like it had for 35 years in the classroom. So young. So innocent. They had just begun their journey; how could they be lost? The teacher in me thought: well, how could I be lost at my age? Shouldn't I have figured things out by now and have "mastered" this whole "life" situation? After all, I'd had plenty of time, money, and other resources at my disposal. Shouldn't those have "fixed" me and everything in my life? We believe that if we have all of these things, our lives should be "perfect." We are conditioned to believe that if things go "wrong," or not the way we want them to, we should just work harder, or longer, or simply get more "things" to fix the situation. More, more, more instead of less, less, less. It doesn't matter how short or long we are on the path either; it just takes one "missed" step or "missed"-take to go reeling off in another direction, off our true path. I thought about what I would tell my young people, my students, and tried to say the same thing to myself: what we have to realize and remember is that life will present the opportunities over and over again for us to learn the lesson we truly need to learn in order to guide us and keep us on the path to our True Self. Learning takes time, and the harder life lessons of humanity take a lifetime.

The priest was an elderly, soft-spoken, gentle man. He called all of the pilgrims up to the altar and embraced each one of us. Love, pure love, flowed abundantly from this gentle man's heart and radiated through his words to our ears, through his arms to our heart, and through his eyes to our souls. Unconditional love. The warmth and glow and energy of it was something that I had not often experienced. I was overwhelmed with emotion and began to weep.

The priest then began to pray, and asked if anyone could translate what he was saying into English. The feelings of unconditional love left me, the magical spell broken as my mind began to build imaginary walls of protection around me. Yes, I *could* translate. After all, I was a Spanish teacher who had spent half my life learning the language. I should have mastered it, right? But... what if I made a mistake? Would I have a do-over? In movies, if there is a mistake, they just shoot the scene over again until it's right. Any mistake is just that...a missed take, attempt, opportunity. We all have the opportunity to do another take on things. It may not have exactly the same characters or context, but we can change our lenses and gain a different perspective. "Lentes nuevos." Put them on, and try again. Focus and see things more clearly. But fear of vulnerability and shame clouds our lenses and keeps us from even trying to see the possibilities. We create an illusion, then focus on the speck marring the lens of our cameras. We keep rubbing and rubbing at it, trying to make it go away.

And so was my experience with learning another language. No matter how proficient I got at speaking the language, I was still afraid of that moment when I would make a missed-take, conjugate a verb incorrectly, use the wrong word, or forget a word altogether. Here, weeping in the Cathedral of León, I froze with fear of being found out as an imposter Spanish teacher.

I have since learned that this irrational fear of publicly being "found out" is called "imposter syndrome," and that several high-achieving, successful people have admitted to having these feelings: Maya Angelou, Tom Hanks, Emma Watson, Neil Gaiman, to name a few. I can't help but contextualize this in the education system. As we set higher and higher expectations for children and expect more and more perfection, feelings of imposter syndrome will continue to grow among our young people, and with it, greater feelings of anxiety. As the Buddhist teacher Pema Chödrön says,

"We need to learn to fail well," and hold that feeling and grow from it. The feeling of "failure" is uncomfortable, and we will do and tell ourselves whatever it takes to avoid it. But "failure" is a human experience that happens to everyone, whether we want it or not.

As it was, a vivacious young lady from Scotland stepped up and volunteered to translate. The priest began. He spoke slowly and enunciated clearly. It reminded me of how I spoke to my students in the classroom. As she translated, the Scottish lady displayed some emotional distress as she struggled to find the "right" words to translate what the priest was saying. But that magic spell of unconditional love fell over her when the priest looked her in the eye and held her hand. He gestured and acted out what she didn't understand until she could give a "loose" interpretation of the meaning of what he wanted to communicate. Not a literal translation, word-for-word. She interpreted the overall feeling and meaning behind the love in his message. He talked of following your own path, listening to your own heart, being kind and gentle to all, and urged us to have faith, always forgive, and live the grace of God. Now I was really sobbing!

This is what I tried to do as a teacher for my students, but that I couldn't do for myself as a teacher. Why is it that we can give of ourselves so generously to others, yet not to ourselves? What conditions had to exist in order for me to love myself like I had loved my students? When would I let go of the fears and let myself be free to be me, unconditionally?

The next day, I decided I would like to see the Parador de León, which is featured in the movie "The Way." The Parador is where they shot the scenes for the luxury hotel that the characters stayed in and treated themselves to some much needed self-care. Parador comes from the word "parar" in Spanish, meaning "to stop," and is the name given to historic buildings, monasteries, fortresses and castles in Spain that have been converted into hotels managed by state-run companies. Many purist peregrinos on the Camino believe that staying in a parador is "cheating" and too indulgent. After all, the purpose is to suffer on the journey and be able to repent your "sins." How often do we do this in life? Teachers are the absolute masters of it! The belief is pervasive and persuasive: if I am not giving 200% every day, in every moment, including the evenings and weekends, then I am not a good teacher. If I am not the last teacher there in the evening and the first teacher there in the morning, then I surely am not doing enough to get an A, let alone the ultimate goal of an A-plus!

In all fairness, though, this expectation is not simply a self-imposed mental conjuring. The practical demands on teachers are so great that we *have* to put in all those hours, just to tick all the boxes of requirements and accountability placed on us. ...or do we? Is it an ever-prevailing attitude and expectation in society today since the advent of computers and data in our lives? We measure everything, and nothing—NO THING—is enough. We translate that to ourselves and those around us. The data, standards and checklists are constantly running through our brains like a ticker tape of information and data that is supposed to drive our actions. Keep moving, keep going or you'll never get there! As a result, we do not "parar." We do not take breaks for self-care, like in the characters in *The Way*. And as a result, we continue to suffer.

But in the film, once the characters stopped at the parador and treated themselves to the much-needed self care of a hot shower, a comfortable bed, and most of all, rest, they were able to reflect on their journeys. They appreciated the beauty and grandeur inside them and around them. They broke out of the prison of their minds and began to heal the cells of their being through sanctuary and cloister. Humans need this to heal and move forward. Yet in the classroom, we push all students along the curricular path, whether they are ready or not, and give them little to no time for reflection and finding the true meaning in what they have learned. And it is the same for the teachers. Teachers don't have enough time or opportunities for sanctuary and reflection on what is "holy"—*whole*-ly—and important for themselves and their students in order to create a safe learning path for all. We are forcing teachers into PLCs (Professional Learning Communities) without first allowing them enough time for reflection on their own teaching situation, their own goals, and the best practices to reach their goals. They are not allowed to be themselves and think about what that means in the bigger picture of education.

When I arrived at the Parador of León, it immediately stopped me in my tracks. I stood before it, gazing up at the huge, majestic and impressive structure, imagining not only the movie being shot there with famous Hollywood actors, but also all the kings and queens of Spain who had likewise passed through those hallways. As I was attempting the typical tourist thing of taking a selfie in front of the Parador, a lovely lady with dark hair and sparkling dark eyes came up to me and asked, "Would you like me to take your picture?"

I was taken aback because she looked like she was Spanish, but I was surprised to hear her speak in perfect English with no trace of a foreign accent.

"Yes, please!" The conversation that followed was magical. Her name was Liliana, from Puerto Rico. Upon learning her name, I smiled. Lilies are my favorite flower. It wasn't until later that I would realize the significance of lilies that summed up this person who would become my guiding angel on the Camino. The symbolism of the lily is profound and widespread throughout all cultures and religions. In Christianity, it symbolizes rebirth and resurrection. For alchemists, it is a moon symbol representing femininity. Ancient Greeks and Romans included it in many myths and legends. The lily has a dual meaning in Chinese culture, being given at weddings because its name sounds like the start of a phrase wishing the couple a happy union for a century. At the same time, it is given to those who have experienced a recent loss because it is believed to help heal heartache.

I explained to Liliana that I was a Spanish teacher and that I had left teaching. After a few minutes of chatting to get to know one another a little better, I felt like I had known her a lifetime. She, too, would be journeying along the Camino, and she asked if I wanted to walk with her and her husband, Jaime. A flood of emotional relief poured over me, and I immediately replied, "You are so kind—yes please, I would love that!"

She invited me in to meet Jaime and take a tour of the Parador, which was reserved for guests staying there. I learned that the Parador was originally the Convento de San Marcos, a convent, sanctuary, and hospital for the poor and for the pilgrims on the Camino. It also housed the Knights Templar to protect the pilgrims on the Camino, and later was a concentration camp for those opposing Franco in the Spanish Civil War. Such a conflicted purpose and history behind the intentions of such a holy place.

It's perhaps fitting, too, that the Parador's original namesake, Saint Mark, authored the second Gospel, which emphasizes the importance of learning and applying spiritual lessons. I had already learned so much about the history of the Camino, from my classrooms in both the U.S. and Spain. But, as it's always been, the real and meaningful lessons of the Spirit would begin when I actually walked the path. The next day, I was going to meet Liliana and Jaime outside the Parador to start a journey that would span a lifetime.

8

Lessons learned

8.1 Personal Reflection Activity

When you are struggling to do something and you have failed, who is your little "angel" that helps you get through it? What is this person like, and what do they do to help you? This person is here to help us blossom into our best self in the garden of life. Imagine this person as a flower and fill in the blanks of these characteristics.

8.2 Interpersonal Connection Activity

Text or call the person who is your "angel" and thank them for ways in which they help you blossom and grow.

9

WE MUST GET REAL TO SURVIVE

"The truth may be stretched thin, but it never breaks, and it always surfaces above lies, as oil floats on water."

— MIGUEL DE CERVANTES, *DON QUIXOTE DE LA MANCHA*

AFFIRMATION:

I always know what is real and what is not when I get real still and listen to the whispers within.

"Have you ever lived or studied in a Spanish-speaking country?"

I was asked this question a lot in my career, especially when I was teaching classes for business communication. Sheepishly, I had to confess my perceived "sin." No, I had not lived or studied in a Spanish-speaking country. I used to turn red with the heat of embarrassment and shame; a deep, dark secret about me had been unearthed. My ego would flare at the thought of such judgment that I was "not enough" because I had not actually traveled to a country where they spoke the languages I had studied and was now teaching.

So, fuelled by the desire to be enough in the eyes of others, I finally took my first trip to Spain and France at the age of 28, with my husband. We decided to leave our three-year-old daughter in the care of her grandparents, which was a painful decision for me. I look back now and see how powerfully I was motivated by the will to become a "real" language teacher. I felt the only way to receive validation was to travel and experience the target cultures I was teaching about.

Whether or not it made me a "real" language teacher is probably besides the point. It was, as nearly all travel is, a life-changing experience. I had spent years of formal education studying *about* the target language and the culture. I could write an almost perfect essay in Spanish about the adventures of Don Quixote, or in French about Le Moyen Âge. I felt really good about what I knew and could do. After all, I got straight As and had won numerous achievement awards that—falsely—validated my skills. It was a perspective and a validation from outside of me. But this was how I measured my proficiency. I also put a lot of value in the number of red marks I had on my papers…the fewer red marks, the more I knew and the smarter I was, right?

Well, when I got to France, I faced a whole new reality with my language skills. I was knowledgeable about all the monuments and history and facts and figures I had learned in my French classes. I had a deep understanding of how the French culture and language worked around me. However, I lacked a crucial skill: I could not communicate the feelings, needs, or desires I had within me. If the other person did not know the other half of the dialogue I had memorized in my French class, then I was tongue-tied. If I was not in a similar situation or context that went according to the script or facts that I had learned from the book, then I was frozen with fear, uncertainty and humiliation robbing me of my ability to speak. I was so disillusioned and disappointed like Don Quixote when he met the Knight of Mirrors. (I wasn't kidding about that essay!)

How could this be? I had studied so hard. I had done everything asked of me and got straight As. I was not a failure! But even as I told myself this, I was now living in the "Real World School" of humanity. Like many students, I was feeling the disappointment that my formal education had not properly prepared me for what was being asked of me. Sure, life lessons are the most powerful, but do we really have to wait until we leave formal schooling before real, personalized, and meaningful learning can begin?

My experience in Spain was marked by a similar dismantling of my confidence. My husband and I had missed a flight, so I had to take up communication with the very stern-looking Spanish lady behind the counter. I tried explaining to her that I had just missed my flight, doing my best to sell her my sad story of why I had missed it, and convince her to book me on the next flight at no additional charge. At first, she would have no part of it! I didn't even know how to say "I missed my flight!"

Somehow, though, in that moment, my vulnerability kicked in. Unmoored from my textbook Spanish knowledge, I began emotionally communicating from my heart. I didn't know the exact words from a script, but I used the ones I knew to plead my fear, frustration, and desperation. Crying, of course, added a lot to the interpretation of what I was going through. I was also saying things like "I LOVE SPAIN, and I want to see more of Spain and get to know better the beautiful people and their country! I have studied Spanish for so many years, and I just want to travel here to learn more!"

Through those words, a heart connection was forged, and she finally agreed to issue me a new ticket at no charge, of course with a lot of directions on how not to miss my flight again in the future. I was so grateful and felt something I hadn't felt before in my interactions with native speakers: a human, heart-to-heart connection. It was calming and hopeful. I hadn't been corrected for my grammar mistakes or misuse of a vocabulary word. At one point, she asked me "Qué plaza quiere, Señora?" to which I quickly replied "No, no! No quiero ir a la plaza!" Then, realizing that in this context, "plaza" didn't mean the town square, but rather "seat" on the plane, I said "Oh, número del asiento," to which she replied "Sí, claro." We both laughed.

From that first trip outside the country, my learning from real world experiences through travel and integration in the target cultural context was real, meaningful and personal to me. I would return to France, Spain, and many other countries after those initial trips and take an empty suitcase to fill with... well, "trash," as my daughters sometimes teased me. But for me, it wasn't trash—it was treasure. This "realia" was a way to bring other contexts back home to the classroom, for students who didn't have the opportunity to travel abroad. Brochures, plane and train tickets, receipts, maps, empty food packaging... there was very little "trash" that I wouldn't save with relish.

Back in my classroom, I used this realia to create learning centers that would provide my students with opportunities to have real world interactions with the target language and culture. I took my own experiences as a motivated but intimidated language learner, and used them to shape the ones I wanted my students to experience in the classroom. I only used the textbook as a reference, not as my curriculum. I taught around themes and contexts from what one might experience as a person living in that country. Real-life situations: at the market, traveling by train, plane, bus, or metro, booking accommodations, visiting historical monuments, museums, or sites, using the phone, going to a restaurant. We used props, played "make-believe," and problem-solved real-world obstacles. I asked them leading questions to help them figure things out when they inevitably got stuck, as all learners do when they're practicing. Ultimately, we experienced the language through our senses, attitudes, and emotions. This was the awe-inspiring "affective domain," which I had discovered was a powerful medium through which to learn and grow in knowledge.

Eventually, I began taking students on trips into the target culture so they could experience everything firsthand. During the school year, we took field trips to nearby places that afforded the students the opportunity to interact with native speakers, but also see with "lentes nuevos" the impact that immigrant communities have had on the majority culture. We Venn-diagrammed everything between the target language and culture and our own personal language and culture, in order to make connections and grow deeper understanding. What resulted was almost always an appreciation of differences through our similarities—making that human connection.

We brought our real world experiences from field trips back to the classroom and explored them even further by writing about them, talking about them and sharing them with others, much like we do every day with our personal experiences outside of school. It made learning alive for the students, and live on in their mental landscape. It created heart memories that were more powerful than any exercise or activity we could do in the textbook. This shared humanity deepened the connection between my students and me, but more importantly, between my students and their peers. I tried to create a safe environment for students to take learning risks. We created a culture of family and community, and "we are in this together."

Every Monday, as the students entered the classroom, I stood by the door with a basket. As each student entered, they would pick up one of the items from the basket. Each item was numbered, and that number determined where they would sit that week. The numbered item also contained directions for a conversation in the target language with their new "compañero/a"—their partner and companion for the week. This forged a path to connection between the two students, and allowed them to get to know each other better. It also empowered students to become teachers themselves, to share their gifts and strengths with others. To lift them up and show them the way. To allow their light to shine in a one-on-one comfort zone, instead of in a cameo spotlight when they're called upon by the teacher...usually when they weren't paying attention, or were distracted with some personal challenge like not enough sleep or not enough to eat or not enough support at home...*not enough*, there it is again!

Over the course of my career, I taught in private and public schools. I taught all ages, from 3-year-olds to 83-year-olds. I taught Spanish, I taught French, I taught math. I taught businessmen and healthcare workers and twelfth graders and my own daughters. But no matter the language, no matter the school, no matter the location or decade, one thing that held true: we all learn better through connections and content that is personalized, meaningful and real world...that touches the heart and comes from the spirit.

When I first set foot on the Camino, in the aftermath of so many truths that swirled into uncertainty, this was the one I knew I could trust to guide me. I had lost so much of my sense of purpose, my sense of self. But this conviction in the power of making connections in the real world shone the way forward on a darkened path and guided me to the first steps of a life-changing, life-affirming journey.

9

Lessons learned

9.1 Personal Reflection Activity

Think of your favorite subject in school and possible careers related to that subject. Create or find a print or video advertisement for a prospective job in that field.

9.2 Interpersonal Connection Activity

Talk to a friend or family member about what your strengths and interests are and brainstorm possible career fields that might be a good fit for you, and why.

Then, reach out to a company in that field and ask if you can come visit and see their operation firsthand.

10

OPEN WOUNDS

"Within ourselves, there are voices that provide us with all the answers we need to heal our deepest wounds, to transcend our limitations, to overcome our obstacles or challenges, and to see where our soul is longing to go."

— DEBBIE FORD, AUTHOR

AFFIRMATION:

I must always take a step in order to move forward and see more clearly the path ahead of me.

I didn't sleep much the night before my first day on the Camino, since my mind was caught up *thinking* about starting my first day on the Camino. It reminded me of the first day of school. Mixed emotions of both excitement for a new year and another "beginning," but also nervous about the unknown. What would my students be like this year? How many students in each class? How many preps? Was I prepared? What would I change about last year that didn't work? What could I "fit in" this year that I didn't get to last year? Did I have enough materials and resources to do what I wanted/needed to do? Did I need to start working on a grant or writing a proposal to the PTA or do a fundraiser to get the money to buy what I needed for my students? What would my Professional Development Plan (PDP) be this year? How was I going to prove to the "powers that be" that I am an effective teacher and that my students are "worthy?" How many AP students would I have, and how many would pass the exam this year? How many passed the exam last year, and was that enough to not feel ashamed that I had let down my students and my principal? What school grade did we get, and what demands would be made on us this year based on that? Who left over the summer? Will there be any new administrators? What would the parents be like? Will I have any that will give me a hard time? What are the new teachers like? Is there anyone new in our department? Are we all going to get along? You can see why sleeping was a long shot.

All this noise going through my head was driven by fear of the unknown, or fear that I wasn't enough, or fear that I didn't have enough or do enough. It was the same for the Camino. Did I have everything I might need, plus other "just in case" stuff? Had I researched, studied, and prepared enough for every possible situation based on what I had read on forums and in books based on other people's experiences? Why was I doing the Camino anyway, and what did I expect to get out of it? How many others had completed the Camino? How many "failed" and didn't make it? Who am I going to meet along the way? Will they be kind and friendly or will they judge me? What will I do if I get lost or left behind? The "monkey mind" of fear.

Already, the very first "official" step I would take on the Camino was one burdened with a pack full of "whats," "whys," and "what ifs." A pack of worries that would weigh me down. But it's human; it is what we do. We take every fear from the past AND the ones about the future and put them in a pack on our back that we carry with us through life, and we trundle along like pack mules.

On the Camino, this is represented by rocks. It is the tradition to pick up a rock that is the size and weight of the burden or worry that we are feeling, and to carry that rock until we have worked through the problem. When we relieve the emotional burden, we no longer need to carry the rock with us as a symbol. Then, pilgrims leave them on the stone signposts that mark the way on the Camino. Or some leave them in piles that grow into little hills daily. It's beautiful to walk along the Camino and see so many rocks left behind, and know that the people who put them there felt they could finally let go of them and move forward, unburdened.

So even before I took the first step on the Camino, I had stuffed my pack full of metaphorical "rocks"—not to mention my actual enormous backpack I would have to carry. The next morning, I was so nervous and sleep deprived that I felt sick to my stomach. I couldn't eat anything or even drink coffee. I didn't want to drink too much water because I didn't know when I would reach a place where there would be a bathroom. I didn't want to have to pee along the way where others might see me!

The first part of the journey from León is less than idyllic, compared to what one might imagine for the beginning of a spiritual pilgrimage. It took us through the industrial side of León and across a busy interstate. Fuel for the fear. On I walked, one foot in front of the other. But as the day wore on, the temperature rose to over 30 degrees Celsius (90 Fahrenheit). To match it, my monkey mind heated up with the conditions, and the hot energy in my feet rose too. Blisters began to form, but instead of stopping and taking my boots off and letting my feet breathe and dry out, I kept going. I didn't even say anything to Liliana and Jaime. I didn't want to hold them back; Jaime had already said that he wanted to do four kilometers per hour in order to get to the destination by mid-afternoon. This would coincide perfectly with siesta time and happy hour, also the hottest part of the day in Spain (hence why it is siesta time and happy hour!).

All the questions in my head were like a bull horn during a pep rally, but they were not cheering me on. WHY was I wearing hot, heavy boots and wool socks in 90° weather? WHY did I let that guy sell them to me? WHY didn't I do more research? WHAT am I going to do if my blisters keep getting worse? WHAT can I do to prevent getting more? WHAT will happen IF I get lost? WHAT will I do IF I can't keep up with Liliana and Jaime? WHAT IF I can't finish? WHAT will people say IF I have to come home after only one day?

With the luxury of a calm mind, it's easy to see that these panicked questions are based more in emotion than fact. Of course, in the moment, it's a different story—and of course, in that moment, I wouldn't possibly be thinking about how my situation related to grammar structures in Romance languages. But please, bear with me as I indulge in my Spanish teacher side and deliver a lesson on a dreaded grammar topic called the "subjunctive."

Mastering the subjunctive is considered by many language teachers to be the pinnacle of success, yet it is also the bane of their existence. They struggle with teaching it in a way that the students can understand it enough to use it properly. Students don't really struggle with the mechanics of the subjunctive conjugation, but rather with the *concept* of when and how to use it. How do you *communicate* using the subjunctive? We don't use the subjunctive much in English anymore, so there is no direct method of correlating how to use it in Spanish to how we use it in English.

Like with most concepts in education, especially languages, the standard approach is to give the student a list of rules and examples and then ask them to imitate or reproduce them. "Drill and kill" worksheets are the lesson plan. "Don't worry about how to apply them in the real world—that won't be on the test!" This works to a certain level, but does not go deeply enough into the heart of learning in order to completely understand and "own" it. When I taught the subjunctive, I made a concerted effort to try a different approach. Let's see if it works with you...

There are two "moods" in Spanish: the indicative and the

subjunctive. The indicative is straightforward. It does exactly as it says, it INDICATES —or "points out," in grammar terms—a statement of fact. When learning a language, we start first with the indicative mood and learn to make "statements of fact." We can plot them along a timeline of present tense, past tense, future tense, maybe even like a math teacher with a graph or a history teacher with a timeline. Our mind does this every day; it creates "statements of fact" to indicate actions or events that occurred in either the past, present or future. I ate an apple...I eat an apple...I will eat an apple. The indicative mood is very linear, logical, and quantifiable...something we can "trust" as evidence, so it must be true! Unless we are talking in terms of "The Matrix," the indicative mood is in REAL time, a definitive point on that timeline, and thus, reality. Easy enough, right?

So what about the other "mood" we use to communicate: the subjunctive? Well, the subjunctive is a mood of wishes, desires, and hopes. Things that may or may not be real, may or may not be true, may or may not happen. It is the mood of emotions, and in my interpretation, weaves in and out of the timeline. It cannot be definitively pinpointed on the timeline; it's not in REAL time, and therefore, is not REALity. I *may* eat an apple. I *might* eat an apple.

In the classroom, I would draw a timeline and ask for students to give me statements of actions and events. Of course, they would give me simple ones like: "I went on vacation to Spain," or "I ran a marathon," or "I got an A on my Spanish test." I would ask them when these events occurred, and we would plot them on a timeline. Then, I asked them to give me some ridiculous statements, and they would say things like "I ate a worm," or "I won the lottery," or "My parents gave me a brand new BMW." These statements could be true, or maybe they weren't true. Most likely not. So, we could not pinpoint these on the timeline. These statements were couched in a concept of emotional reality— hopes, dreams, fears, expectations, desires, wishes—and with that comes a lot of DOUBT.

Doubt creeps into the subjunctive mood in more than one way. Using the subjunctive depends somewhat on whether the hopes, dreams, wishes, and desires are for oneself, which can likely be in one's control, or for another, which isn't controllable. For example, if I say, "I want a new BMW," that is the indicative, a statement of fact. If I say I want it, then it must be true for me, and therefore, it is irrefutable. But! If I say, "I want my parents to buy me a new BMW," then it's something else entirely. The concept is that we cannot control others and what they do, so there is a lot of doubt in what I've just said. Therefore, we must use the mood of the subjunctive.

In short: if I want something, it must be true, because it is in my mind and the controllable reality that I create in my mind. It's basically a statement of fact, and easily identifiable on a timeline. However, if I want someone else to do or be something, I have no control over that. I need to place these ideas in the realm of doubt and uncertainty, somewhere above the timeline: in the subjunctive.

I can't help but speculate why the subjunctive fell out of use in English. It used to be correct to say, "I want that my parents may buy me a new BMW." "May" and "might" are relics of the subjunctive in the language. But now we use the infinitive: "I want my parents to buy me a new BMW." Grammatically speaking, it removes the doubt. Does this "indicate" that we believe we can control others? Or maybe we think that we *can* control our own destiny if we believe it enough. Want it badly enough. Try hard enough. Set enough goals. Have enough resources. (Enough, enough, enough.)

So, how'd I do with the subjunctive? You're probably incredibly relieved that we don't use it in English.

But even with its abstractions and complications, thinking in terms of the subjunctive mood was incredibly applicable to my predicament on Day 1 of my Camino journey. Incessant questions ran through my head, and my attempts to answer them could be sorted into facts and emotions. Things that may or may not be true. Realities, and wishes.

WHO is that walking ahead of me? *It is Jaime.* Fact. Indicative.

WHAT is Jaime doing? *He is trying to make me walk four kilometers per hour.* The subjunctive. But my mind goes further...

WHY is Jaime doing that? *He is mean and doesn't care about me.* Another emotion, a story I make up to feel better about myself. I just want to feel like what I am doing is enough, so I plunge into the victim mode. Here, I'm not responsible for my choices or behaviors or results, because, after all, those are not my standards I am living by, but rather, the standards of some person outside of me that I can now blame for my perceived shortcomings!

Our coping skills deteriorate until we do one of two things. Either we put an inadequate bandage over the wound and let it fester until it goes deep into our souls and becomes part of our DNA. Or, it is a constant irritation to our being and is a source of pain and suffering that is easily triggered by any sort of "rubbing" up against people and situations. As my hot feet slide around in my heavy boots, desperation rising, it is impossible not to imagine all of my wounds as sensitive, inflamed blisters.

But despite the doubts, the emotions, the wishes, facts remain: I am doing my best, and my best is good enough based on who I am, what I have been through, my age, my experience, my goals, and so on. But I, like so many, often get lost in the struggle and the story of believing we're not enough. I didn't prepare enough. Other people steered me wrong about what shoes and socks to wear. I was a fool for thinking I could do this. I am going to fail.

It is not reality. Moreover, on the first day of the Camino, I allowed it to rob me of living in the reality of the present moment. I couldn't enjoy what was really going on outside of me. I didn't marvel at the little things that greeted me that first day: hundreds of sheep being herded through a busy street blocked off by policemen, the terrain stretching into countryside as it left the city behind, the little church of the Virgen del Camino with the Virgin Mary surrounded by the twelve Apostles...so small and beautiful, yet so cherished, significant and meaningful to the area, like all of the little treasured memories we hold inside of us.

10

Lessons learned

10.1 Personal Reflection Activity

Write down three things that happened to you today. Write down three things that you wanted to happen but didn't. Write down three things that someone wanted you to do. Write down three things that you wanted someone else to do. Place these events in the appropriate box below.

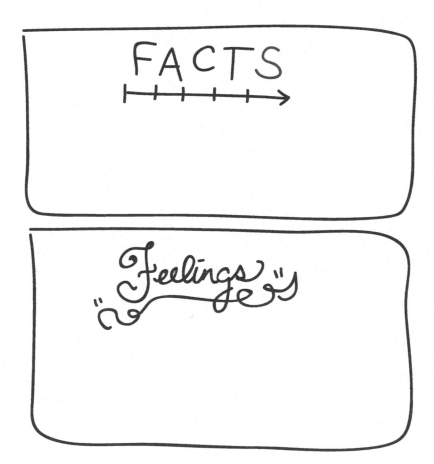

10.2 Interpersonal Connection Activity

Place the information from your Personal Reflection on the timeline below and use it to tell a family or loved one about the day you had today. Be mindful of what parts of your day were reality and which ones were feelings and highlight that in your recount.

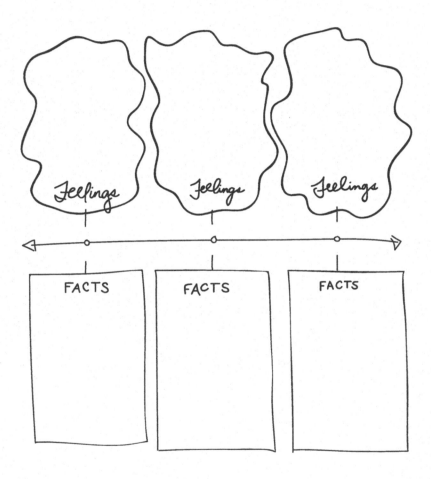

11

FOLLOWING RECIPES

*"Real education should consist of drawing the goodness and
the best out of our own students. What better books can there
be than the book of humanity?"*

—CÉSAR CHÁVEZ, ORGANIZER & ACTIVIST

AFFIRMATION:

*I am the chef of the recipe of my life, and as chef,
I can choose all the special ingredients that will go
into the "pièce de résistance" that is me!*

Despite the blisters, and the heat, and the monkey mind, I successfully made it to my first overnight at Molino de Galochas, approximately 30 kilometers (18 miles) from my starting point at the Parador de León. It was an old mill that was used to harvest and grind grains, now renovated as an accommodation for peregrinos. The place was decorated with a collection of old "galochas," an old style of wooden shoes designed to wear in the muddy fields to harvest the grains. It was run by a lovely couple, Máximo and Mercedes, who spoke very little English, but who still communicated to all pilgrims through their actions from the heart. Mercedes gleefully and lovingly shared the history of the mill, the shoes, and the surrounding area with visitors. She saw that I was struggling to walk because of blisters, so she took me by the hand and led me to a stream running behind the Molino.

She told me to relax, take off my boots and wool socks and stick my feet in the icy cold water. It was like heaven. Immediately the suffering of the day melted away, and I was overcome with emotion. I had made it. I was safe and enjoying the little pleasures of life again. Rest, good food, good company, good conversation, shelter and nurturing support.

Mercedes had prepared a feast using the food grown in the garden she and Máximo had so lovingly cared for. At dinner, one of the pilgrims, an Irish lady who was traveling the Camino with her sister, said that she had never had the "tarta de Santiago," a special cake made in Galicia with powdered sugar sprinkled on top in the image of the "cruz de Santiago," the Cross of Saint James. The next morning at breakfast, another feast, there was a freshly made tarta de Santiago for all to enjoy. Mercedes proudly shared the recipe and told us all her secrets on how to successfully prepare a delicious tarta. She also explained the origin and significance of the tarta and the image of the cruz de Santiago. There were many "oohs" and "ahhs" and "mmms" as she spoke, not only for the savory cake, but also for the connections and epiphanies that the pilgrims at the table were making between the cake, the Camino and life's essential ingredients.

Lesson plans are kind of like recipes, and teachers are the bakers of learning. There is a list of ingredients that are essential to the creation of the end result we want to create. For example, to make a cake from scratch, we must have certain key ingredients as a foundation: flour, sugar, butter, water or milk, and baking powder. Without water, the other ingredients will not bind together. Without baking powder, the cake won't rise. Without sugar, the cake will not be sweet.

As teachers, we know what these essential ingredients are to a lesson plan. There are basic concepts that we know are needed to build a foundation of understanding and learning. More often than not, today teachers are given these "recipes" by state standards and district initiatives. There is little allowance to make their lessons their own. In the case of the tarta, there are embellishments and details that make it different from other cakes. These distinctions are personal: its unique flavor is a result of almonds and lemon, the products grown in abundance in Galicia. The powdered sugar "cruz de Santiago" that tops the cake is unlike most icings; rather, it's a symbol of the culture and history of the region. The end result is not only a delicious tarta, but also a great deal of pride, tradition and knowledge that is shared and passed on to others within and beyond the Galician community.

So why standardize the "recipes" of learning from state and district mandates? What's the larger purpose of this, how did we get here, and what is the effect of these standard recipes on teachers and students? How has education changed, for both educators and learners, in the last fifty years?

I will extend a disclaimer, here, that I am not an expert on education reform. All the same, my teaching career spanned four decades of firsthand experience in the U.S. education system, from the classroom to the district, to advocating for world language education face-to-face with state and federal lawmakers. Although my experiences are certainly not universal, I witnessed —and was subject to—the shifts and dynamics in the system.

In the 1970s, when I first began teaching, the United States experienced economic decline and high inflation. There were long lines at gas pumps, high interest rates, and a weak dollar abroad. The U.S. was not necessarily "on top" of the world economically, and many began to point the finger at public education. To review potential issues and recommend action items, a cabinet-level panel, the National Commission on Excellence in Education (NCEE), was established in 1981. The panel gathered data and produced a dramatically titled report, "A Nation at Risk: The Imperative for Education Reform."

From where I sit, this was the beginning in a long trend of leading with the "shadow side" of education. Fear, negativity, pessimism, anger, resentments, jealousy and frustration reigned. The report even went so far as to state, "Our nation is at risk.... If an unfriendly foreign power had attempted to impose on America the mediocre education performance that exists today, we might well have viewed it as an act of war." (It's on page 5, if you're really interested in slogging through the original document.) So now, education is a strategy of war? School is a war zone of conflicts, battles and strategies, simply to "win?" Win what? I never have figured it out.

As a result of this shift in attitude, schools began to focus more on academics and preparing students for college, perceiving that we needed a "better" workforce. High performing "employees," perhaps, rather than "workers." As more money was poured into this reform, results was demanded to make sure the investment was worthwhile. State governors got more involved with educational reform, as they were being held accountable for the funding their states received. By 1990, many governors joined President George H.W. Bush to establish measurable goals for educational reform in this country. They called these goals "America 2000," as an outline for the next ten years of education standards.

The goals the panel agreed upon are basically the groundwork for today's education policies:

"By the year 2000...

...all children will start school ready to learn.

...the high school graduation rate will increase to at least 90 percent.

...all students will leave grades four, eight, and twelve having demonstrated competency over challenging subject matter including English, mathematics, science, foreign languages, civics

and government, economics, arts, history, and geography. Every school in America will ensure that all students learn to use their minds well, so they may be prepared for responsible citizenship, further learning, and productive employment in our nation's modern economy.

...the nation's teaching force will have access to programs for the continued improvement of their professional skills and the opportunity to acquire the knowledge and skills needed to instruct and prepare all American students for the next century.

...U.S. students will be the first in the world in mathematics and science achievement.

...every adult American will be literate and will possess the knowledge and skills necessary to compete in a global economy and exercise the rights and responsibilities of citizenship."

By the mid-90s, I was teaching in Florida, which released its own report, "Blueprint 2000." (Looking back, we were collectively very obsessed with the New Millennium, weren't we?) Florida's Blueprint 2000 gathered data with the goal of improving schools and student performance. Among other things, the report stated that businesses wanted students to graduate with skills that were rising in value in the 1990s. Emphasis was placed on developing skills necessary to become "information managers" and "resource managers," as computers were becoming more prevalent, and "more responsible employees," with initiatives addressing attendance rules.

It was also decided that since we were a "nation at risk," we needed to set standards for teachers and students alike. Here we are... the dreaded recipes! By that point, I was intensely curious about the end results of this plan, and wanted to contribute my own voice—input from an actual classroom teacher—to the final product. So, I worked on the committee that developed the first standards for world languages in Florida.

You may be thinking, "How could you have helped write the very standards that have come to inhibit teachers so much? What about the almonds, and the lemons, and the powdered sugar cross design?"

To that, I would say, standards are good as a reference. Standards can help you identify those essential ingredients for a tarta, and inform whether or not the end result should be sweet, sour, or maybe even salty. Standards are a helpful resource for teacher planning, but they are not intended to be used as a law, or a commandment, or a measure of worthiness in the world.

But more often than not, standards are passed down to teachers to be memorized and followed to the letter. Some go so far as to give directions and a script on how to deliver the lesson, so that all teachers and all students are doing the same thing, at the same time and in the same way. The goal is to "make a cake." The same cake. No different flavors, or ingredients, or decorations that make it our own, created from our passions and gifts, customized for our students' appetites and strengths.

Meanwhile, as we eagerly moved into the New Millennium, yet another initiative rose up from the stoked fears of "not enough." No Child Left Behind (NCLB), a 2001 federal policy, was largely driven from the interpretation that we, "as America, the most powerful nation in the world," were ranked "behind" other countries, based on test scores of high school students in math and science. (I should note that the use of quotes here is to denote perception, not citation.) NCLB operated on the shadow side of scarcity and lack. It not only promoted competition among states and schools for federal funding, but this competition also trickled down into subjects, teachers, students and schools. What were the more important subjects; who were the more worthy teachers? Which students were at risk of being left behind? Which schools performed well; which schools were dragging down?

This culture of measurement and competition naturally

resulted in the estimation that there were too many "bad teachers," that were not preparing students. It was the first time I saw and felt fear in my administrators and colleagues, as well as the students. The fear of not being enough, the bitterness of being reduced to test scores, the shame of American students coming anything other than first on the world stage.

Despite its best efforts, NCLB was still not getting the desired results. During the Obama administration, education reform evolved into Race to the Top (RTTT), which established even higher standards, more "rigor and relevance" in the curriculum, and more accountability through increased standardization and data-driven evidence, that of course corresponded to Federal funding. End-of-course exams were established for all subject areas, as well as stringent standardized teacher evaluations that were based on the theories of just two "experts," either Robert Marzano or Charlotte Danielson.

This "one-size-fits-all" mentality was promoted in an effort to streamline results and measure data, but at the same time, teachers were being asked to differentiate instruction, teach innovative "out-of-the-box" thinking, and make special accommodations for "special needs" students with individual educational plans (IEPs). Now, it was No Teacher Left Behind. School grades, Annual Yearly Progress (AYP), Blue Ribbon Schools and countless other recognitions were established in an attempt to validate teachers, students and schools.

It was during the back-to-back policies of NCLB and RTTT that I was teaching at a School of Choice followed by a district supervisor job. The environment of competition and achievement only grew during those years, pressurizing learning environments and workplaces. STEM subjects—science, technology, engineering, and math—were thrust into priority, as more research showed that the U.S. needed to be competitive in growing industries and global economy. The arts, world languages, and physical education were cut from many programs. District staff, school administrations, teachers, and students: all were expected to achieve more, to do more, to be more. To get more accolades and more recognition, in order to receive better school "grades" and more funding.

And now, we have the Every Student Succeeds Act (ESSA), and schools are ramping up to compete for the federal funding once again. Meanwhile, all the baggage of the past 40 years of education trends and policies weigh heavy on the human beings struggling to perform in the system. The practical existence of surviving every school day is an arduous path for teachers and students alike, as they feel they must walk across flames and jump through hoops every day.

This is not working. The classroom curriculum has become complicated beyond recognition. Pedagogical trends in education change like fashion trends on the runways in Paris, New York, or Milan. Teachers wonder if they should be modeling the pedagogy of Vogue, Versace, or Prada in their classrooms this year, as administrators come to capture one of their teaching moments as they "strike a pose." Is this "haute education" at its finest?

Nearly every teacher I talk to these days feels overextended, demoralized, and exhausted. So many teachers are sick of having their hearts broken daily, hands tied by the bureaucracy of education. They are sick of not truly being able to do what is best for themselves, and the children they so lovingly teach. They want to teach from the heart and not from a checklist of standards. They want to meet each child at the place they are at this point in their development, regardless of data and rigor and standards.

Moreover, they want "their children" to flourish and grow in a safe and nurturing environment that meets each child's needs, and not the needs of people outside of that child and their context. They want to feel respected, valued, and empowered to learn and grow into the next higher version of themselves as a teacher, and not compared and shamed for never being or doing enough. They want love, belonging and joy for themselves and "their children."

Despite this overwhelming disconnect between their wishes and realities, teachers still muster up the energy to weather the stormy and rough seas of the school day when they would rather run away. And many do. According to recent government data, teachers are leaving the profession in unprecedented record numbers. About 50 percent of new teachers will leave the profession within the first five years of teaching. And, the number of young people studying to become teachers is down 42 percent. There is a real crisis in education.

Many are abandoning the profession because it's too prescriptive, too demanding. There are too many formulaic recipes that don't resonate with teachers, or are too hard to decipher. There is no freedom to make our own cakes. Yes, it's important to set out with a shared goal, and planning recipe-lessons is most effective working backward from the intended result. However, we may all agree that the goal is to make a cake, but we don't necessarily agree on the ingredients, nor the "right" steps to make it. Some people mix the dry ingredients together and then add the wet ingredients. Others mix it all together in the same bowl. *"Blasphemy!"* cry the recipe purists.

But we all still end up with a cake, which was the goal. Where education gets lost is in prescribing the perfect cake and expecting teachers and students to recreate that perfect cake. In many cases, that cake that is the standard cake with no personal flavor, like the regional ingredients that make the tarta de Santiago unique. We preach innovation and creativity, but do not practice it. We say that everyone must make a cake and has the right to make a cake, but then, we take away their freedom to decide the process of making the cake, based on individual teacher strengths and student needs. We shame them and tell them they are not enough if the cake is not perfect or if they didn't follow our recipe.

All teachers should have the freedom to make their own tartas for their own pilgrim students seated at their table. The only thing education should be requiring from the teachers is that there be certain best practices and strategies for all stakeholders: the essential ingredients that will create the BEST cake for each of their students to savor, that will nourish their hungry and curious learning souls. Things like kindness, compassion, empathy, joy, gratitude and love. When I think back to the tarta de Santiago that Mercedes served, what was memorable was her kindness in making it and sharing it personally with her guests. These are the real secrets to successfully serving up any recipe!

11

Lessons learned

11.1 Personal Reflection Activity

Find a copy of a basic cookie recipe that you like. Circle the ingredients that you love. Think about what special ingredient(s) you might add to make this recipe your own.

11.2 Interpersonal Connection Activity

Share your recipe with a friend and find out what theirs is. Fill out a Venn diagram comparing them. What ingredients do they have in common? What's different? Why? How does this cookie make a statement about you?

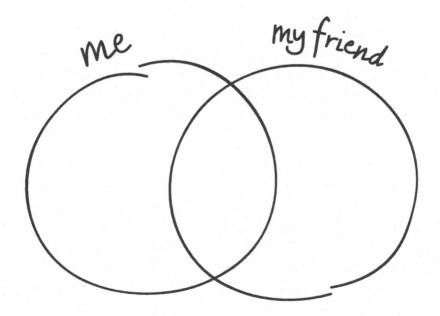

12

GOALS, STANDARDS AND THE "TRUE" PEREGRINA

"This above all, to thine own self be true, and it must follow,
as the night the day, thou canst not then be false to any man."
—WILLIAM SHAKESPEARE, *HAMLET*

AFFIRMATION:

I set the goals, standards, pace and rewards that are
valuable and most essential to the learning journey I
am traveling at this moment in time.

On the second day of my Camino journey, I made a somewhat foolish choice out of fear: I agreed to backtrack several kilometers in order to meet up with Jaime and Liliana so that I wouldn't have to walk alone. They had stayed overnight in town, whereas I had chosen a quaint old mill house in the country that had a lot of culture and history to it.

The "what ifs" were still chanting in my head, spawned from all my online research. Reading forums and message boards and blog posts had equipped me with knowledge and worry in equal measure. I had read about vicious stray dogs, violent storms, and pilgrims who'd died along the way. One story had stuck out: four months before I arrived in Spain, a woman from Arizona had gone missing on the Camino. Horribly unable to push this from my mind even before I departed, I'd read so many online posts that speculated what had happened to her. My family had raised serious concerns about safety because of this story. And now that I was walking the same path she did, it was impossible not to think of her. Hope that she would be found safe and alive. Worry about the possibility of something similar happening to me. So, I traded the physical comfort of fewer miles and wear and tear on my feet for the mental comfort and physical safety of walking with other people.

Well, the Universe always gives us the lesson we need to learn, and that day was no exception. As we were walking across a farmer's field of corn, a bad thunderstorm moved in. The sky turned black. Lightning cracked nearby, and thunder rumbled on its heels.

In these conditions, the mind's first instinct is to hustle. But I was a slow walker then, and I was extra cautious about keeping my footing. One slip and I could fall and break something, completely ending my chances of finishing the Camino! I had brought walking sticks with me, but this was Day 2; I was still awkward and not very proficient at using them. So I tried to stay calm and take my time, but there were slippery rocks underfoot, and soon I found myself struggling and trying to avoid them. If the farmer from the corn field had been watching me, he probably thought I was doing hopscotch on the path rather than walking.

Then the skies opened up. Jaime and Liliana, who were of course ahead of me, walked faster and faster until they were no longer in sight. I had been left behind. There was no place to seek shelter either. I walked as fast as I could, but the storm was growing stronger and coming closer. As lightning was flashing on the horizon, certain death was flashing in my brain. Suddenly my brain cast me as the main character in a movie. Is it a comedy, where I'm in on some cosmic slapstick? I could so easily hear the panicked words of Chris Tucker in the action-packed climax of *Rush Hour 2*: "*Lord Jesus, I don't wanna die!*"

Or maybe I was in a horror movie? Flashes of Freddie Krueger went through my mind as I hurried past rows and rows and rows of corn fields. All of a sudden, there was a rustling in a corn row ahead. I faltered, and watched. Time seemed to stretch into slow motion. Surely this was a suspenseful thriller, then. I stood rooted to the spot, frozen in fear and unable to move.

Finally, from the rustling corn row emerged a figure—three figures! A farmer with two massive dogs, both Mastiffs, each flanking him. I just stared at them, still terrified, thunder and lightning raging around us.

Then he called out to me. "Señora, sígame!" ("Follow me, ma'am!")

Should I obey? Where would he take me? Was it wise to follow a stranger alone in a corn field in Spain? I thought of the woman from Arizona again, and feared all the worst possibilities. But my gut kicked in, and so did my feet. I rushed behind him and the dogs to a nearby shed that I hadn't seen, hidden by the rows of corn. *Oh no, a shed!* Now my mind cued up a movie reel of slasher films.

The farmer could tell I was afraid. He seemed afraid too, as he tried to communicate to me in patchy English. When I replied in Spanish, his fears were allayed. A big smile came over his face. As the shed protected us from the elements, we talked more, and I saw he was kind and gentle—not unlike the Mastiffs. (They were once bred as war dogs because of their size, but today, Mastiffs are actually gentle giants, considered kind and courageous. We all should channel our inner Mastiff!)

Realizing I was safe, I returned the farmer's smile. He told me that when a storm moves in, he comes out to the Camino to check for pilgrims and help them. It is his land, and he allows the pilgrims to walk through it. Even when the skies are clear, he says, it's important to help those who are passing by, one human being to another. The Camino traverses many private farms and lands, and the attitude is the same with all of them. Many farmers and landowners will leave food on a table for pilgrims to have, with a cup and sign that says "donativo" (donation). Some give back to the Camino and serve it and the pilgrims in amazing ways.

Whenever I reflect on this practice of complete strangers, I am humbled by the kind gesture of humanity and reminded how we are all weathering our own personal storms every day. The hand of a "gentle giant" reaching out to lift us up is priceless. Asking how someone is as you pass them by is kindness manifested. Listening with a heartfelt intention of hearing what they say opens the connection to the heart.

We all have bad days and storms to weather. In my career, I witnessed teachers and students struggle with "what was going on at home." Yet there are so many demands in the classroom. So much to do, so many expectations, so much energy used. It's nearly unthinkable to tack on additional stressors beyond our control: a sick child or parent, our own illness, a lack of money, a lack of food, an unstable home, verbal or physical abuse. All of these problems set our minds in motion, consuming all our energy and even knocking us off our path.

Imagine a professional environment where administrators recognize storm clouds gathering over their teachers, and stop by their classrooms to help out, or ask how they're doing. A kind word, a loving gesture, empathy and compassion can go a long way to get someone back on path and give them hope to keep going. After my encounter with the farmer, I was energized and able to finish the day, even though I was still struggling with blisters and heat rash creeping up my legs.

That night, I went to a local store and got more bandages for my blisters. I discovered that treating blisters is an art form on the Camino, and everyone has tons of advice as to which ones are the best. One of my lessons on the Camino became "501 Ways to

Treat Blisters," but the hardest part was figuring out which one was the best for MY blisters, MY feet and MY context. That's what all learning and life experiences are about, right? What works for other peregrinos may not work for me, and vice versa. But as I stood there, intimidated by the extensive display of bandages that took up half the tiny store, I realized I simply needed to try some out. There were other pilgrims there, also stocking up on bandages, so I heeded their advice and chose the ones most of them recommended. If they didn't work, I could always try another kind.

I returned to my hotel, showered, put new bandages on my blisters, and went down for dinner. The conversation was abuzz with news about an Irish lady who had to be rescued on the Camino. I soon realized that they were talking about the Irish sister who had asked Mercedes to make a tarta de Santiago! I had seen them only that morning, when I departed Molino de Galochas. Had Edith gotten stuck in the storm? What happened to her sister Dolores?

Edith was walking the Camino with her sister, Dolores, and it was evident that Dolores did not really want to be there. She was suffering terribly and could not keep up with Edith. In truth, the conversation between them at Mercedes's dinner table was painful for me to listen to. Edith was the older sister, quite stoic and confident. She was traveling the Camino with only a bottle of water to signify that she didn't need anything but water to survive. Metaphorically, she was not going to take on any burdens, especially of others, and was, therefore, not going to carry a backpack or walk with anyone else. This struck me as odd since she had invited her sister to walk the Camino with her, yet didn't really walk with her. Why did Edith agree to Dolores tagging along if she knew she was going to walk alone?

Apparently, Dolores had expressed extreme concern over Edith's decision to walk with just a bottle of water, especially in the

90 degree heat. But Edith dismissed her pleas and in turn, shamed Dolores for being weak and having no willpower or strength to accomplish her goals. "That's been your problem your whole life, and that's why you've never gotten anywhere!" Edith had told her. The whole dinner party radiated discomfort at overhearing them, and I suspect there was also a morsel of relatability in the sisters' dynamic. That feeling of being shamed into doing something for someone else that we really didn't want to do, but that we felt we had to do in order to prove our worth and our love for them. It seemed appropriate and sad that Dolores carried a name that means "many pains" in Spanish. It can also mean "sorrows." How can we find joy and live in peace if we are choosing sorrows?

According to all the buzz among the peregrinos, it seemed that Edith had passed out from heat exhaustion. She was probably delusional and had wandered off path to find water or someone to help her. She didn't have a cell phone, and her water bottle was empty. Dolores, who was walking way behind her, passed by and didn't see her. When Dolores arrived that night at the hotel, Edith wasn't there. So, some locals went out to look for her and found her lying unconscious in a field. They rushed her to the hospital. Dolores was wracked with guilt about the situation, beating herself up for not being there for Edith. The fact that she came on the Camino was evidence that she was there for Edith. But she couldn't control Edith's choices, nor could she suffer the most serious consequences of Edith's choices. Those actions and results belonged to Edith alone. So, instead, Dolores suffered worry, guilt and shame in the relationship. It's a difficult thing to hear, but ultimately those were her choices too.

Frankly, I could relate to both of the sisters. Dolores's persistent worrying rang true, as did her willingness to take on the burdens of others. But I recognized myself in Edith too. How many times had I stoically and pridefully pushed through something when in reality I needed to slow down? Instead of taking a break, practicing self-care, I would ignore any instinct my gut was offering me, and identify the help I needed, let alone seek it out. Was it help from someone else? More sleep, more rest, more fun, more time, more... what, exactly? Yet I pushed on with my metaphorical "bottle of water" into a vast field of perceived obligations, keeping my eye on what I thought was the horizon—the end point, the goal—only to find out that it was merely a mirage, and I was delusional.

Nothing is truly urgent. Nor will we "burst into flames" if we don't finish everything that we have on our proverbial plates. There's also not a reward for having the fullest plate. Life is not, neither personally nor professionally, an all-you-can-eat buffet. Why do we load up our plates, or worse yet, allow others to pile their helpings onto our plates? So many teachers do this, including me. It's the Ego, urging us to earn a badge of honor for our suffering. *I've got a degree in this that says "I know everything!" I've got this. I don't need any help. I am strong and capable and in control. I will not be vulnerable.* The truth is, we are vulnerable every single day. To protect ourselves, we fill our water bottles with the eternally flowing words of: "The more I do, the more I am and the more successful I will be."

Thank God Edith had been found and would survive. But the relief at her safety didn't stop my mind from telling me, "I can't do this. Look at what happened to Edith." Suddenly, I felt very vulnerable. When dinner broke up, I found Liliana and broke down, sobbing about my struggles and my doubts. She comforted me, and encouraged me with words of loving kindness and hope. She and Jaime had walked other parts of the Camino in previous years, she said, and they had struggled a lot, but they made it, in the end. She was much the better and happier for having made the journey. That is all I needed to keep going.

Maybe it is all any of us need to keep going on our path in life: hope, encouragement, and knowing that someone else has also traveled that path before you, and made it.

12

Lessons learned

12.1 Personal Reflection Activity

You and your best friend are going to visit Walt Disney World. Choose a park and create an itinerary of things you are going to do at the park, based on a) how much time you have, b) weather, c) what you each like to do, d) past experiences, and e) research and suggestions from others.

12.2 Interpersonal Connection Activity

Send an email to a friend or loved one of your proposed trip and itinerary to a park in Disney World. Ask for a response from them by email or by phone with details of what they like and what they want to change in your proposed itinerary. Be sure to listen and ask questions to better understand the needs and wishes of your friend/loved one who might (hypothetically or in reality) be going with you.

13

FALLING FROM GRACE

"Turn your wounds into wisdom."
—OPRAH WINFREY

AFFIRMATION:

I know deep inside myself that there is no failure, but rather only Faithful Attempts In Learning.

There are many etymologies of the word "grace," according to the Online Etymology Dictionary. From Old French, *grâce*: pardon, divine grace, mercy, favor, thanks, elegance, virtue. From Latin, *gratia*: favor, esteem, regard, pleasing quality, good will, gratitude.

How much grace exists in the classroom—or in society these days, for that matter—in any of these interpretations? Thanks to current educational reform, it has become very difficult to sustain mercy, elegance, virtue and regard in the current climate. There is very little that is pleasing and agreeable.

In my life, these negative emotions reached their peak when I thought I was at my peak: when I left the classroom after 31 years of teaching and started a job at the district level in a supervisory position. As the World Languages Resource Teacher, it became my job to help implement and enforce No Child Left Behind (NCLB), Race to the Top (RTTT), and eventually Every Student

Succeeds Act (ESSA). But really, in my teacher heart, I felt like everything was so wrong. What I felt in the pit of my stomach every day was a different acronym: UGH! *U Go Home! You don't belong here!* But, where was home? I was off path and not living my truth.

I had been enticed by the district job because my quixotic spirit convinced me I could be a champion for world language teachers there. I believed I could advocate for the profession, that I could be a source of inspiration and guidance to teachers like I had been to my students. What I encountered instead were even greater roadblocks—an overwhelming culture of "no, we can't" rather than "let's find a way." There were so many "experts," yet so little wisdom, so little greater understanding.

The divide between "us and them" was as wide as the Grand Canyon! There was hardly any camaraderie, gentle guidance, or loving spirit. Instead there was a "top down" leadership model that propagated fear and negativity. It was a culture of "never enough" and "I know best." We were managers and distributors of knowledge, but not partners. We were trained in "Strengths Finder" and "The 7 Habits," but were not held accountable to their practices. We worked in cubicles with no view of the outside world—an ironic detail not lost on me, then or now.

Most of us working at the district had good intentions, but our hands were tied by fear. Fear that we would do or say something that would be picked up by the public and made into a shaming headline. Fear that we would not get adequate funding for initiatives and projects that we deemed essential to teacher and student success. Fear that we might not have all the answers and look incompetent.

When I first started my job at the district, I was struggling with sitting so much, so I asked for a standing desk and laptop. No money. I asked for a different chair. No money. I asked to attend conferences and take teachers to conferences. No money. I asked to go out and visit teachers in their schools, to which they replied, "Why would you need to do that?" I really was supposed to be at my desk, just in case they needed something or by some *Twilight Zone* happenstance, some official from the state called with a question. My attendance was required at many, many planning meetings to share ideas and the latest news coming out of the Florida Department of Education (FLDOE) in Tallahassee. We made action plans, but were always met with too many roadblocks. No money. No resources. No time. No buy-in. No interference with the principal's power. No. No. No.

There was obviously a pecking order as well. The core subject areas were the most important, got the most funding, and wielded the most power. As a world languages educator, it was difficult to deal with feeling sidelined and overlooked—especially knowing that an effective world languages curriculum can integrate core subject areas with language learning.

Eventually, we were allowed to visit teachers in schools, which I was very excited for. I could visit old colleagues and new friends and actually help them! To lift their spirits, I made up goody bags of chocolate tied with fancy ribbon and a tag that featured an inspirational saying, like "I hope your year is full of sweet rewards." I gave goody bags to the principals with gold coins in them that said, "Your language teachers are a real treasure. I hope you discover the hidden jewels in each one." But I never actually got to see a principal, and always left the goody bag with their secretary. Why wouldn't the principals see me? After all, I thought, I was there to help. I was there to advocate for the teachers and world language education. But their guards were up—both figuratively and literally. I was not getting past the staff at the gates of the front office fortress. After all, there is always a perceived "war" on something, and we are in defense and sometimes battle mode in education.

Moreover, there is very little trust between teachers and

the district. Anyone could be a spy, an enemy, a traitor, a whistleblower. Teachers often believe district staff are out of touch with the realities of the classroom, and simply want to prescribe or criticize from their "ivory tower," unaware of what may or may not be effective—or even feasible!—in practice. Each interaction with the district could yield yet another "flavor of the week" initiative that was designed to receive more funding.

When I visited the teachers, it was very much the same. I came to their classrooms with an arsenal of standards, checklists, articles about best practices, strategies, and of course, the latest initiative coming down from the state. My directive from the district was to foster "vertical alignment" in the world languages programs and to get the teachers to collaborate and play nicely together. Well, I might as well have been sent in for peace negotiations in a war zone.

I was getting nowhere, except for stuck in the middle of a power struggle generated by the Ego and its fear. I suppose I had experienced that from time to time in the classroom, when students didn't "obey" me or do what I had asked or expected. Mostly I had seen my role as a teacher more like that of a facilitator, and therefore my relationship with the student and their parents was more like a partnership.

After my first year at the district, I decided to take a different approach to visiting the teachers. I had to build trust, and find a heart connection like I had done with my students. I would still go bearing gifts like chocolate and snacks, but I also went with the intention of service and the gift of curiosity. I offered to grade papers, put up bulletin boards, talk to the students in the target language, or even teach a lesson, if they needed it. I was curious about their classroom experience, and asked questions that tapped into their "school spirit." Questions like: "Why did you become a teacher?" "Who was your favorite teacher, and why?" "What is your favorite thing to teach, and why?" "What do you want most for your students?" "How are you, and how is your family?" "Have any travel plans?" "What's new? Tell me what's going on in your world and if/how I can help." Slowly, but surely, their hearts opened too. I listened, I hugged, I cried, I laughed, I graded papers. Understanding and empathy took over.

For many, I became more of a teacher therapist, an equal partner, a friend walking beside them and holding their hand. I loved it, but it also wore on me, emotionally. I was powerless to do anything to help change their situations or stop their suffering. My empathic heart absorbed it all, and there were negative effects. I started having trouble walking.

I had experienced many health issues since I started working at the district. I tried a slew of countermeasures, like exercising at the gym every day after work, acupuncture, energy healing and reiki, herbal therapy. I put on 40 pounds and felt terrible emotionally and physically. I was armoring up to protect myself better on the "battlefield."

Turns out, the body is wise. The things you believe, the emotions you are experiencing, both past and present, will manifest in your body. The helplessness I was feeling. The failure I was feeling. The heartbreak that I was feeling. I couldn't do anything to change what was going on for the teachers in the schools. I could not save programs or their jobs, which, district-wide, had been cut by 30% in three years.

My legs started to give out on me for no reason. The doctor tested me for multiple sclerosis and amyotrophic lateral sclerosis, more commonly known as MS and ALS. When he told me that I would probably be using a wheelchair in five years, it was like a bolt of lightning had struck me, and I knew exactly what I had to do. I needed to get out of that job. But I couldn't go back to the classroom. I was too weak and too sick and too humiliated. My spirit was broken, and I felt hopeless. So I made the painful but necessary choice to retire early from the once beloved and noble profession that had been such an essential part of me, and that had once brought me so much joy and meaning.

•   •   •

Before long, I was lost.

Lost. Lose. She who loses. That which is lost. From Old English, *losian*: to be deprived, destroyed, unable to find or even fail to win.

According to etymonline.com, by the 1600s, the word "lost" came to mean "spiritually ruined and inaccessible to good influence." This certainly felt apt. My spirit was ruined, and I felt totally isolated from anything good or positive. Unsure how to move forward in healing my heart, I spent three years in physical therapies and treatments to get my health back. I started walking on the beach every day and doing tai chi. I rested and exercised in balance, and tried to practice self-care. But what about the intangible healing of mind and soul?

Even though I had retired, I felt like I still had much to contribute and give back. I decided to continue working with professional organizations, and I attended conferences. This had been a normal part of my career in the classroom, and seemed like a good way to stay involved with the profession I loved so much. However, something happened at the first conference I attended after retiring that would break me wide open and start me on a journey of self-discovery.

As at all conferences, I checked in and got my name badge, which I promptly put around my neck. As I mingled with others at the conference, chatting with new people and even some acquaintances who didn't quite remember my name, I noticed them look down at my name badge. Then, they said to me: "Retired?! Well, why are you here if you are retired?"

I was shocked by people's reactions to that word, which ranged on the emotional spectrum from "jealousy" to "shame" and "unworthy." When I had filled out the registration, I didn't have any official "title" to put in the part of the form that said "title" or "affiliation," so I left it blank. The conference organizers had contacted me and asked me about where I worked, and I said I had retired. So, that is what they put as my "label." The official title that defined me and who I was, by tethering me to what I did.

I let the question "Why are you here if you are retired?" get under my skin. *Who am I, then, if I don't have a title? WHY, exactly, am I here? What is my purpose now?* It became even more awkward and painful during meetings or conference presentations, as we went around the room and each person introduced themselves. Everyone else stood, chest puffed out and head held high, and proudly declared a title of who they were. I thought, "Am I not worthy of being here because I have no title?" That was the impression I had. I also got the feeling that since I was retired now, and not actively suffering through the trials and tribulations in the classroom, others thought that I had no clue and nothing to contribute. At one point or another, these words were actually said out loud.

For years, I had served on many state committees for establishing standards and creating assessments for both student achievement as well as teacher certification. Yet, as soon as they found out I was retired, they seemed to dismiss me. The name badge that hung from my neck felt like a label that deemed me unworthy...*not enough*. It was a scarlet letter of shame that became a burden that I no longer wanted to bear. It made me vulnerable to judgment and feeling like I didn't belong.

In an effort to deflect, I started introducing myself with some multilingual vocabulary humor, thanks to the Spanish word for "retired"—"jubilada," which means "jubilant" or "rejoicing." I would say, "I'm not retired! Retired makes it sound like I'm tired over and over again. I'm jubilada... rejoicing! Feeling joy over and over again."

But it was not true. Inside, I was not rejoicing. I was still lost and suffering in my life. I was still strongly identified with my Ego and all of the "things" that I associated with my sense of identity... my accomplishments, my titles, my accolades, my perceived power to control things, my fears.

So, after that first conference, I came home and asked myself the question: "If I am not my title or my job or my accomplishments, WHO AM I?" I continued to look for answers outside of myself. I listened to podcasts and read books and took online classes about spirituality. I meditated and kept a gratitude journal. Someone, somewhere had the answer. I just knew it. I had been lost, and here I was, seeking. I thought I was doing all the right things to find my answers. I created mantras and "best practices" of how I wanted my day to unfold as it aligned with my vision and purpose. But I still felt like I was NOT there YET. I would soon learn the power of "NOT YET" in the learning cycle.

I would later come to realize that "quest" and "question" are related in so many ways. Our learning must be a "quest," or an adventure to find answers to life's big questions. This journey cannot be defined by one person, nor one event, nor one point in time. It truly is like a path. Every answer leads to another question, which is just another step in the direction of another answer, and so on. Sometimes we get off path. Sometimes we get lost in the woods. Sometimes, we trip on things on our path and fall down. But the path is always there, and it is always our path... no one else's.

It turns out an actual, physical path was beginning to call to me. As my 60th birthday approached, I began thinking of what I could do to commemorate the occasion. And concurrently, in my meditations, I began having visions of returning to Spain and walking the Camino. My dreams were filled with images and faces from my experiences in Santiago de Compostela some fourteen years earlier.

So when the dreams began, I knew I had to go back to Spain and follow my heart along the Way of St. James. I decided to go alone, much to the objections of my family. They were afraid I wouldn't be safe. They wondered what would happen if I got lost or hurt and they weren't there to help me. They wanted to protect me and keep me safe. That's what we think love is, but it is really just the opposite. It is letting go, in faith and prayer, and allowing for the freedom of what is to manifest. No matter what happens, good or bad, there is a lesson to be learned and growth to be made. It is the learning journey we're all on, in the classroom and beyond, on the paths of our lives.

13

Lessons learned

13.1 Personal Reflection Activity

Think of a time when you experienced failure. Write a letter to that younger version of yourself in which you console and give helpful advice that will inspire.

Dear Me,

_____

_____

_____

_____

_____

_____

_____

_____

_____

_____

_____

Love,
Me

13.2 Interpersonal Connection Activity

Get a box and place five things in the box that you feel best represent obstacles you have faced in life. Then, with a partner, take turns removing items from each others' boxes and asking questions to complete the chart:

OBJECT	OBSTACLE	WHY?	HOW?	ADVICE OR OTHER IDEAS?

14

CLIMBING

"Owning our story can be hard, but not nearly as difficult as running away from it. Embracing our vulnerabilities is risky, but not nearly as dangerous as giving up on love and belonging and joy—the experiences that make us the most vulnerable. Only when we are brave enough to explore the darkness will we discover the infinite power of our light."

—BRENÉ BROWN, RESEARCHER & AUTHOR

AFFIRMATION:

I give myself permission to only reach as high as my arms can stretch from where I am at this point in time and in this place where I stand at this moment

Just a few days out of León, the terrain of the Camino begins to climb, eventually reaching the highest point at Ponferrada. Before long, I started struggling with the ascent. I was wearing out muscles in my legs that I didn't even know existed, and I soon felt disheartened by the fact that I was already challenged in only the *beginning* of the climb. There were still several days of ascent ahead of me!

I fell further and further behind Jaime and Liliana. Liliana would walk slowly enough to keep me in sight, like an angel watching over me, but Jaime stuck to his goal and kept his pace of four kilometers per hour. He was growing obviously frustrated with Liliana lagging behind him. At one point, after waiting for me to catch up, he simply remarked, "You should have trained more before you came on the Camino."

These words, of course, stung. How quickly we are to judge someone when we do not know their context, where they have come from and what they have gone through. Our frustration or ignorance can cause us to judge and react too soon. Maybe that's why Steven Covey says: "Seek first to understand, and then, be understood."

How was I supposed to train for mountains in Florida? I had prepared as well as I could for long distances. I would get up at 5:00 am and walk the flat beach near my house, with the goal of building up to 20 miles per day. Someone had suggested that I also walk over the bridge that leads to the beach area, but it is a busy road that leads from Orlando straight into Port Canaveral's cruise terminals. Thousands of tourists drive over that bridge every day, and I did not think it was safe to walk over it. I didn't want to get killed and never even make it to the Camino at all!

But it was also late spring in Florida, and getting increasingly hotter by the day. My outdoor walking options became limited because of the temperatures and the early evening thunderstorms. So I started walking at the mall with all the senior citizens who were getting their morning exercise. I was no "spring chicken," but I was inspired by them and envisioned myself "still going strong at their age." Something of great hope for me, since a couple of years earlier I had visions of myself in a wheelchair "wasting away to nothing" and slowly dying a painful death and never seeing my loved ones again.

I pushed on past the seniors and through the monotony of doing what seemed like a million laps, past the department stores and the empty food court and the sunglasses kiosks. Walking at the mall, I could never get past 12 miles per day, because I "didn't have the time," or "I got bored," or "had other more important things to do." I armed myself with a small portfolio of excuses I used to rationalize my decision of stopping before my goal of 20 daily miles.

Of course, now that I was on the Camino and my lack of stamina had become an obvious hindrance to my companions, the shame and defense of these choices rose up in tandem. I was so indignant and offended by Jaime's judgment. How dare he be so insensitive? He hadn't been in my shoes leading up to the Camino. He hadn't struggled through the experience of getting so sick I could barely walk, and here I was, walking the Camino, blisters and all! After all, those were my medals of honor. My bloodied badge of courage, right? I had already noticed that when peregrinos would stop and chit-chat with each other, they would exchange statistics on the number and severity of blisters they had, like they were battle scars that clearly demonstrated how much they had suffered, and how much they should be recognized for their efforts. Here on the Camino, blisters were treated like the gold stars we strive to achieve in school, or the number of titles we collect in our email signature.

But the truth is, no one's worth is measurable in blisters, gold stars, or titles. Moreover, we never know the journey another person has taken. This is the power of context. My current context? I was operating on about three hours of sleep per night and 10 hours of walking per day in 90 degree heat. My body was exhausted and needed a break. My blisters needed time to heal. By then, my toenails were beginning to loosen and come off too. Raw, open wounds, like the one Jaime had touched on with his course comment.

I hadn't done enough. I wasn't enough. I was a failure. We are not trained to separate what we do from who we are, and therefore, we equate what we do to who we are. I am my blisters, I am my gold stars, I am my titles. I am supposed to be better than this. I am not supposed to fail. But here I am: failure. This monkey mind continued to chatter at me as I struggled to walk. Burdened with an enormous pack stuffed full of emotional rocks I couldn't seem to let go of. I did not want to continue on the Camino any more because I felt like I wasn't enough. The weight I carried got heavier and heavier, until half an hour outside of the next town, I nearly collapsed. I could not take another step.

The shame and desperation closed in on me, and I began sobbing. I was literally having a meltdown, probably physically from the heat, and definitely emotionally. Liliana told Jaime to call a taxi to come get me. I stopped mid-sob, and began refusing. The voice in my head screamed, "NO! NO! NO! I CAN'T TAKE A TAXI OR I WON'T BE A TRUE PEREGRINA!"

If I took a taxi, I would be a fake. I would be cheating, a cardinal sin in the world of education. Things were not going at all as I had planned and expected and envisioned and dreamed. Disappointment and disillusion had an overwhelming choke hold on me.

•   •   •

I had planned for the Camino as if I were doing a lesson plan for school. After all, I'd had an entire class on it fourteen years earlier, which I passed with a grade of "sobresaliente" ("outstanding," since in Spain they don't use the A through F grading system). According to many educators, that meant that I had achieved "mastery," right? Ha!

To start the planning process, I dusted off my notes, combing through them in search of fine details that would help me map out my journey. In education today, for lessons, we "unpack the standard." This starts with circling the nouns and verbs in this description that was created by someone else of what is "normal." The standard might have read something like this: "Student will be able to communicate and interact with cultural competence in order to walk the Camino Francés and arrive at the Cathedral in Santiago de Compostela."

The objective? To walk the Camino. How long should I spend doing that? How long do I have? How long does it take others to do it? A month. Can I be away from my family for that long? Would I need more time than that? If I only have a month, I will have to hurry, and what if I can't do it? I'm not sure if my body is strong enough yet to put it through all of this. What if I fail? How will I face everyone? I can't be a failure! Maybe I shouldn't even go. I can't do this.

How do I get there? When will I go? I would love to go during July, alongside many pilgrims planning to arrive in Santiago on July 25, to celebrate the Feast Day of St. James with all the other pilgrims and festival-goers. But I don't love crowds, and Spain would be hot in July. I started doing research online to find the answers.

Do I have to do the whole thing? I read many posts about people who start the Camino in St. Jean Pied-de-Port and didn't make it over the Pyrenees Mountains. Further west of the Pyrenees, some people didn't make it through the grueling temperatures and expansive fields of the Meseta. Some got lost and had to spend the night in the woods. Maybe I would just start in León, skipping the Pyrenees and the Meseta both.

Fear started tightening its grip on my gut as I flooded my mind with more and more information from online. In return, my mind was sounding off like a bullhorn at a school pep rally, but it was NOT encouraging like the cheers of school spirit! "You can't walk over the mountains. How will you prepare? There are no mountains in Florida! You were barely walking just two years ago! You can't take the heat any more. You don't want to suffer or worse yet, die! You're a slow walker. You can't finish the Camino in a month. You just can't do it!"

To quell my rising fear, I turned to resources and preparation. This is the part of the lesson plan where teachers think about what "tools" they have in their teaching "toolbox" to implement the plan. Materials and strategies. What would I need to walk the Camino? A backpack, and shoes. Okay, but what kind? There were so many choices in selecting both of these crucial items. More research. More confusion.

Eventually I went to a hiking store and spent six hours trying on shoes and getting a lot of personal attention from the kind and patient sales associates there. I walked up the fake rocks to make sure they didn't slip too much, and trekked around the store to test their comfort. What about socks? Wool was recommended because of their wicking properties to keep my feet dry. Rain protection: poncho, rain jacket, backpack cover, shoe covers, phone protector, etc. Backup battery pack for my phone. Hiking clothes, from hats to zip off pants to SPF-protected shirts. I did laps in the store with different backpacks, stuffed full with various levels of weight to see which one was most comfortable. A camel water pouch, water purifier tablets, a funnel to help when peeing in the woods, sanitizing wipes, tiny rolls of toilet paper… By the time I walked out of there six hours later, my purse was almost $1,000 lighter! But I was prepared, right? I had everything I would need for every possible situation that I might encounter.

NOW, I was prepared. Or was I? I continued to read the blogs, and stuff my backpack fuller and fuller. I was reminded that, yes, there WERE stores in Spain, and that a credit card would not add that much weight to my already overburdened backpack. But I insisted on choosing everything from research and expert guidance—or so I believed. What I was really doing was making choices from a place of fear. Thus, the over planning. I was coming from a place of scarcity and not from a place of abundance.

This is a real mindset in education, a side effect of the intense focus on measurement and performance. There is never enough.

What if I don't have what I need to prove that I am an effective teacher? As teachers, we spend a lot of time planning to thwart these possibilities. The more we plan, the more we can control. The more we can control, the less vulnerability we feel. Less fear. More security. More likelihood that things will go the way WE want them to go.

But here's the deal. The more we plan, the more we place things into a mold or into a box. And when things don't fit into that mold or box, we become frustrated and even angry. We might even have a sobbing meltdown on an ancient pilgrim's path in Spain, as our friend pleads with us to simply take care of ourselves and adapt to our current needs.

Our expectations are pre-determined, and when reality doesn't meet our expectations, especially if they're set too high— like to perfection, for example—we are disappointed. Devastated. Heartbroken. Worse yet, we may not know how to handle those big emotions, and we either numb out, armor up, or run away, just to avoid dealing with them.

I had put myself in a situation where I couldn't avoid dealing with my dashed expectations, deep sense of failure, and shame about "cheating." I was crying on the side of the road in a foreign country, feet bleeding, back aching, emotionally exhausted. My physical and mental pain were in a blistery foot race for my fraying attention. Jaime and Liliana were strongly encouraging me to take a cab the rest of the way into town.

And then, the memory of what happened to Edith popped into my mind like a flash of light. A lightbulb flickered on; the skies parted to "enlighten" me with epiphany. I finally saw the light. It was a no-brainer at that point: I needed to be rescued. I was lucky that I could take a taxi now, instead of collapsing in a field and requiring a search party to find me. That single thought wiped out all the others racing through my head.

I got into the cab and slumped down in the seat so that I wouldn't be seen by the peregrinos who were still able to finish that stage of the Camino. Once I got to my hotel, I took a cool bath and treated my blisters and sore muscles. Then, finally soothed and relieved, I sat down to reflect on the day and write in my journal.

Now, from the quiet refuge of my hotel room, my perspective was shifting. When I thought about the taxi, the voices spoke differently in my head. They were more affirming, reassuring me that I had done the right thing. Sometimes we call it "rationalizing," when we try to make sense of something. We justify our own behavior with logic and plausibility—even if these are not true or appropriate. For me though, I like to think of the Latin root word, from "reason." In Spanish, it's "razón;" in French, "raison." To have reason to do something. Whether others can see it or not, it is real for the person trying to make sense of things that will give them the courage to go on. That reason is a pathway to figuring out what we need or don't need, what we can or cannot do, who we are and are not.

I realized that I did not melt on the spot like the Wicked Witch of the West in *The Wizard of Oz*. I was safely in my room and not lying in a field somewhere. I had not been arrested or punished for taking a taxi. I decided that I needed to do what was best for me, and if that meant taking a taxi when I could no longer continue on my own, so be it.

Though the Camino may have been perceived as a "test," it was not a final exam. Learning has no destination. I didn't "already fail," nor did I even have to consider it "failing" at all. I was there, on the Camino, walking when I could, taking a cab when I couldn't. I was learning so much about the world outside of me, but even more importantly, I was learning so much about the world inside of me. I was not doing it exactly like everyone else. I didn't have the same things in my backpack. I was not going at the same pace. I was not having exactly the same experience or even an ideal, "perfect," A+ experience. Who decides that, anyway? I refused to measure my experience by someone else's standards. I was having my own personal learning experience…a REAL education!

My efforts came with errors and shortcomings, yes. I was literally stumbling and could have done things differently, and, in retrospect, maybe even better. BUT, the reality—REALity—of this life journey was that I was on the Camino, and would simply put one foot in front of the other until I reached my end goal, Santiago. That was enough, and I was enough. My enthusiasm and conviction would be tested and sometimes wane, but my new mantra was courage to keep going on my path. We must seek and be open to the support that is needed to continue on each step of the journey. We must also be the support to others on their journeys. Our shared humanity is a worthy cause, and so is the real treasure that we seek, our own personal grail…our True Self.

14

Lessons learned

14.1 Personal Reflection Activity

Think of a class subject or an area of life in which you are struggling. Name three things you are doing to overcome that struggle. Then, complete a permission slip for each, using this formula:

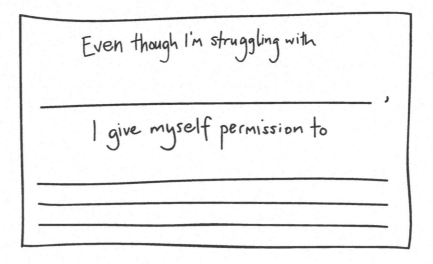

Even though I'm struggling with

_____ ,

I give myself permission to

_____

_____

14.2 Interpersonal Connection Activity

Think of someone you know who is struggling right now. Send them a short message of encouragement (by text, chat, phone call or hand-written note) each day for a week affirming what they are going through and inspiring them to keep going and figure out a way to take that next brave step forward.

15

THE ULTIMATE TEACHER IN-SERVICE

*"The bond of our common humanity is stronger than the
divisiveness of our fears and our prejudices."*

—JIMMY CARTER, 39TH U.S. PRESIDENT

AFFIRMATION:

I am in service to my fellow human beings every day, in every way.

As I left the flat terrain and scorching sun of the Meseta behind, I welcomed the lower temperatures of Galicia. Although the terrain was still rugged and trending upward, the cooler air helped my feet not feel like they were on fire from the heat of constantly pounding them on the ground. With my renewed courage, I tried hard to manage that hot energy that comes from repeatedly doing something the same way. But I was pushing through the pain and suffering, thinking that I might somehow emerge a victorious hero. No pain, no gain, right? At least that is what we are always told.

New blisters were beginning to form on my feet. Even more unknown muscles awakened in my legs, and began to shout at me to slow down even more. The town coming up was the one where the woman from Arizona disappeared. As I climbed higher, my fears returned.

The support system to the Camino in Spain is phenomenal.

So many people give selflessly of themselves to support the peregrinos, and join in the humanity of spreading love and compassion. People set up little kiosks of food for a donation. Some play music and give away fresh fruit picked from their orchards. Folks like my farmer friend keep a watchful eye on the pilgrim's path, ready to help any in need. The Camino route is marked not just with yellow arrows, but also the goodwill of strangers along the path, mapping a kind of route to the heart.

David lives in the middle of nowhere with his partner Suzy. They are free-spirited and loving people who sleep in a make-shift tent and grow what food they need. Every day, they walk to the nearby town, ten miles away, to buy supplies that peregrinos might need on the Camino. It is free to all, but they have a jar for donations that they use to buy more supplies for the next day's pilgrims who pass. They have perfected the practice of recycling kindness. Boomerang goodness.

But there is more to it than that. David literally embraces every single pilgrim who walks by, and today, he is only wearing his underwear. No inhibitions, really! As naked and as vulnerable and innocent as we are at birth. He is so open, warm and welcoming. After each embrace, he asks each pilgrim their name and where they are from. He listens with his whole heart and is affirming and validating. He is offering therapy on the Camino, which reminds me of Lucy from the Peanuts gang, and her roadside stand that says, "Psychiatric help 5 cents. The doctor is in."

David offers up his heart, his ears, his essential being to all who pass. His kiosks hold the gifts of food and comfort to the pilgrims, but he goes beyond. Even the signs above the kiosks are spiritual and healing. "La llave de la esencia es la presencia," reads one. "The key to the essence of life is presence." (Sadly, it doesn't exactly rhyme translated to English.)

David and Suzy practice living in the present moment and fully give of themselves to each peregrino who passes...

wholeheartedly. The light from within them shines brightly and reaches out to bring out the light in others. Everyone feels it. A lighter load through enlightenment, and shining our light on others. We all can and should do that for each other.

What David and Suzy do is not only a service to humanity, but also is rich in Spirit. When I encountered them, it touched the "teacher spirit" in me, that feeling I had in the classroom each day with children. We just needed the basics of wholehearted love, and the openness of sharing the journey together. I didn't need a magic lesson plan or the latest technology or measurable data to prove I was teaching all the standards.

As I reached the town where the young girl disappeared, I thought of David and Suzy and felt calm. The town, Astorga, only has about 50 inhabitants, yet it accommodates hundreds of pilgrims. There are families in the streets laughing, socializing, and gathering in community spirit, something Europeans seem to do well. Contented to simply observe the activities, I sat on a wall nearby and took in the happy energy. A woman who appeared to be American came up and sat beside me.

"Hi, I'm Mary, and I'm a hospitalera. What's your name?"

I was startled, first to hear English, and second to have a complete stranger try to make a connection. But then it made sense, knowing she was a hospitalera. Hospitaleros are people who have completed the entire Camino, then taken a course to certify them as hospitaleros. Yes, there is such a course! The role of a hospitalero can be many things, but the best summary of what they do can be identified in the English cognate: hospitality. Hospitaleros act as stewards of service to peregrinos, performing "host" duties to the thousands of "guests" that pass through on their journeys.

Serving as a hospitalero is a two-week volunteer position, the broad job description of which is simply helping to provide peregrinos with whatever they need. This could be giving directions to the nearest pharmacy, clinic, café, or church service, imparting guidance about the trail ahead, or even lending a shoulder to cry on. There are intangible services like listening and comforting, as well as logistical tasks like organizing meals and cleaning the albergues.

Shouldn't we all be "hospitaleros" on this journey through life? Service to your fellow man to help them along on their journey. A great way to forget about our own problems and serve a higher purpose. To be reminded that as bad as it gets, there is always someone else who has it worse than we do. Get out of "víctima" mode. We all need help at different points in our lives, but we also need to remember that others need help too. It is a sacred human duty to help them, and hospitaleros are a wonderful reminder of that.

Life always gives us exactly what we need to continue the journey…just the right people and just the right experiences. The best lessons from the very best teachers. In that moment, sitting on a wall in Astorga, Mary was the right person for me. I told her my name and immediately began unloading the story of my pain and suffering, of my blisters and sore muscles. I was immediately playing the victim symphony with a full chorus of me-me-me's and I-I-I's. Requiem of the Ego, the perfect soundtrack to my woeful tale.

Mary listened thoughtfully, then offered her perspective. "Look at the people around you," she said. "Everyone is struggling with blisters and sore muscles. We all have our burdens to carry, and it is our job to figure out the best way that works for us."

Still hyper-focused on my own problems, I sang another chorus of whining and whimpering. "I walk too slowly, and can't keep up with others, and they are shaming me into walking too fast and hurting myself, or they abandon me and leave me behind! I'm afraid to be alone."

Very gently, but very firmly, Mary replied: "You have to walk at your own pace, and not that of another—nor should they go at your pace. We are each on our own journey to self discovery. You are never alone on this journey. There is always going to be someone ahead of you and someone behind you. Most important is the person within you. That is the person who is always there to either lift you up and carry you, or bring you down and hold you back. Focus on that person inside of you, and you will never be alone."

Finally, I was listening to her message. WOW, Universe! Hit me over the head with it, will you? Some of our greatest lessons come from our greatest failures, falls and "false steps"—faux pas, a loan phrase from French. And boy, was I having the most profound and meaningful lessons in my life, one step at a time—and I was literally just a few days into the journey.

I stayed the night in a small, family-run hostel, one of only a couple in the entire town. I felt lucky to have been one of the peregrinos to get a room and not have to continue walking to the next town. When I went downstairs the next morning for breakfast, there was a feast laid out on the table. I didn't feel hungry, but the family that had prepared the meal was watching me to see if I liked what they had done. Fresh fruit, yogurt, fresh-baked bread, local cheese, a beautiful place setting with fancy dishes and glasses, a colorful tablecloth, fresh cut flowers. I did notice the little things, and recognized the love that went in to provide them. It was such a great reminder of the power of the present moment and the real gifts of life. *"La llave de la esencia es la presencia,"* David's sign called back to me. This "present" moment truly was a "gift," synonymous in words and concepts.

I gestured to the mother and daughter in the kitchen to come over, and began speaking to them in Spanish, complimenting the feast they had provided. Their faces lit up and their shyness soon turned to excitement. We had a lovely conversation, and already my spirit was lightened by learning about others' journeys and making heart connections. I was not alone. I was grateful. I was nourishing my body, mind and spirit with presence and gratitude for the little things.

I practically skipped out onto the path to start my day, oblivious to my blisters and sore muscles. It was as if I was walking on clouds. I had forgotten all about the woman from Arizona and was actually humming a song. Then, I saw blood. All over the path.

I stopped dead in my tracks, and hoped that it was only an expression, and not an omen. Fear and terror swallowed up all the feelings of gratitude and joy from the morning's gifts. I followed the voices that led me ahead to the source of the blood. There were about four or five pilgrims huddled around an elderly woman who was covered with blood on her face, hands, and arms. Blood had spilled on the ground in front of her.

Amid the hushed melée, I was told that she was 87 years old, and that she had tripped and fallen face first into the ground. There was a steady stream of blood gushing from her nose, which seemed to be broken. The crowd was trying to convince her to get medical help, but she would have no part of it. She was crying and repeating, "I'm so stupid. I should have been more careful. I can't believe I fell. How could I be so stupid?!"

Wait a minute…that was MY self-talk! How did she know what I had been telling myself for most of the Camino so far? The sad truth is that most everyone's self-talk is negative and not nice. I had heard the same dialogue from students for many years, with just a slight alteration: I can't believe I failed.

Well, "failed" and "fell" really are the same, and the difference between growth and being stuck where we are can be found in the gap between our ears. There is where we can truly measure learning gains! The words that we use to talk to ourselves become the mantras that drive all our decisions, actions and feelings of self worth. We often parrot other people's words and expectations, then disguise them as our own. The origin of "not enough." This woman was 87 years old and walking with a fully laden backpack on the Camino. What can get any more competent or awesome than that? YET she was beating herself up for one missed step, a mis(sed)-take. All those other millions of steps she has taken to get to 87 years old did not even count to her in that moment. All those steps of learning gains as she struggled and overcame all odds against her to get to that place right there, right then.

Why will we choose to focus on the one thing we do "wrong" than the million we do right? Why are the only choices black or white, true or false, right or wrong? The red pen from the classroom becomes mightier than the sword in our heads. There is only one right answer. We put an "x" on all the wrong answers and highlight how much of a deficit there is. We deduct points, and establish our worth in a percentage. And then, the grades are measured in comparison to what, and to whom? To other students? To ourselves? To the expectations of someone else who doesn't even know us and the learning path we have been walking?

With the prevalent technology to measure data, we have become a society of minutiae. The bigger picture view is often lost on us. We want to pick at the warts and point out the flaws instead of focusing on the beauty of the whole. One taxi ride is failure. One missed step is failure. Overworked muscles and blistered feet are failures.

Suddenly urged to reassure this woman, I made my way through the crowd and stooped in front of her, gently taking her by the hand. I gave her the warmest smile I could. "You are amazing! 87 years old and on the Camino, unbelievable! We all want to be like you, but we can't follow in your footsteps if you don't get medical attention and make sure you are okay. Let us help you!"

"Yes, yes! Let us help you!" The other peregrinos echoed my sentiment.

She shook her head. "No, I need to keep pushing forward."

A young Italian man took her by the other hand and said, "Here, I will walk with you back to the village. We will just go get you checked out and get you cleaned up."

"I can't possibly ask you to do that. I will be okay. I can go on my own. I don't want to be a burden and hold you back," she said.

"It's no problem," insisted the young Italian man. "It would be my privilege to walk with you and learn from you." With this, the elderly pilgrim finally relented. We helped her up, then she took his arm and started walking back to the village.

The rest of us continued on, and it wasn't long until I was once again lagging behind. I was destined to be "la peregrina tortuga," the turtle pilgrim. After a few hours, I stopped at a store to get something to drink and rest for a few minutes, dearly trying to practice my new intentions. I had just grabbed a bottle of water from the shelf when suddenly I caught a glimpse of the young Italian man in the next aisle.

"Hi," I said, waving to get his attention and hoping he'd remember me. "How did you get here so fast, and where is the lady?"

Recognition lit in his eyes, and he smiled. "I took her back to the village where a hospitalero tended to her. I stayed a little while, but then I left and just walked fast."

"That was so nice of you to help her," I said, relieved.

He looked really surprised at that comment. Then he shrugged. "But that was what I was supposed to do today. My job today was to help her."

He bid me a "buen camino" and was off again, sprinting out the door with his beverage and snack in hand.

I was left gobsmacked. If only we could have that attitude and outlook every day, I thought. For teachers of all kinds, in and out of the classroom. If we could just stop long enough and take the time to sense the needs of others—our students, their parents, the colleagues around us—and in that moment, give what is needed to help them back on their path. Don't leave others behind, but rather go back and pick up the ones who have fallen and give them the support and attention that they need. Journeys like this are not races; there are no winners but the ones who help others along the way.

The rest of the journey to my hotel, I reflected on the kindnesses I had witnessed in just a few short days. David and Suzy. Mary the hospitalera. The Italian man. They imparted to me a profound teaching, earned through experience and personally meaningful to me. I thought about my own teaching, and the kind of journeys I took my students on every day in the classroom. I knew what it was like to be an English speaker trying to learn another language. I understood the vulnerability and the courage required to communicate in a language not "your own." The learning had to be authentic, real, meaningful, and personal in order to be effective. That's why I collected "trash" all those years, and devised learning centers from authentic materials and authentic experiences. That's why I allowed students to explore their learning alone or with a partner. That's why they did projects and worked their way through real world scenarios so that they could figure out on their own how best fit them. That's why I didn't point out when they did stumble or fall when they were speaking. They were showing courage with every unfamiliar word that tumbled from their mouths. Every foreign idea and foreign action that they were willing to risk in order to learn and grow. And I was just there to reach out a hand and lift them up. That was my job as a teacher, and it humbled me and inspirited me and gave meaning to my life.

As humans, we are all teachers and learners, and that is our job together. To reach out a hand and lift each other up, not armor up like gladiators and be ready for attack.

That night, in my hotel room, feet freshly soaked and bandaged, I sat down to do my daily reflections. Reinvigorated by the assurance of the power of helping and learning, I came up with new intentions. This is what I did every day in the classroom after teaching. I reflected on what worked well, and what I should keep, and what was an "improvement opportunity" that I should change and do differently. Sometimes it would work the second time around. Sometimes it didn't. The most important part was to continue seeking a solution. So, I re-solved the problems and set new intentions. I modified my lesson plan—not the goal, just how to get there. I gave myself some "permission slips" and some "can do" statements to guide me along my intentions:

- I can go at whatever pace is comfortable for me.

- I can listen to my body and go with my gut. Take the taxi if needed!

- I can stop for food, water and rest when tired. Practice self-care.

- I can talk to other pilgrims along the way and learn more about their journeys.

- I can be present and en-JOY the journey. Take in the little things.

- I can trust the journey and not be afraid to be alone because I never am.

- I can be grateful for the experiences I am having.

15

Lessons learned

15.1 Personal Reflection Activity

Investigate a problem or need in your community (i.e. unhoused populations, beach litter, elder care). Describe the issue and figure out if there are any organizations already working to address the challenges. If so, what can you do? If not, what can you do?

15.2 Interpersonal Connection Activity

Contact the organization that you investigated in the Personal Reflection activity (by phone, email/letter, or in person). Tell them what skills and support you can bring forth in service to the organization to make a difference.

16

THE IRON CROSS WE ALL BEAR

"Nobody's life is a bed of roses. We all have crosses to bear, and we all just do our best. I would never claim to have the worst situation. There are many widows, and many people dying of AIDS, many people killed in Lebanon, people starving all over the planet. So we have to count our lucky stars."

—YOKO ONO, ARTIST

AFFIRMATION:

I release all regrets and grievances, forgive myself and others for all trespasses, and let go of all burdens in order to lighten my load and my spirit.

Every day I was climbing higher and higher in altitude on the Camino, approaching its highest point at Monte Irago. Here, at over 5,000 feet, there is an iron cross that can be seen for miles. The Cruz de Ferro, literally "the cross of iron." I'm beginning to wonder if it's so named because only those with iron constitutions make it to that point on the Camino.

There actually are many legends and theories surrounding the origin and purpose of this cross (although mine is not one of them, sadly). One legend says that when the Cathedral of Santiago was still under construction, pilgrims were to bring a stone with them, and that when they reached the cross, they were to throw the stone over their shoulder in a ritual symbolizing their journey on the Camino. Some say it was erected by the Celts as a monument to Mercury, the Roman god of merchants and travelers, to mark roads of commerce and travel. And even some say that the cross was placed there by a hermit named Gacelmo in the 11th century, who also erected a chapel, hospital, and hostel there to support the pilgrims on their way to Santiago.

Whatever the origin, it is a powerfully symbolic place on the Camino journey for most peregrinos. Today, the tradition at the Cruz de Ferro ties in with the custom of carrying rocks on the Camino—remember that? Many peregrinos choose to leave the rocks they've carried, as a symbol of their greatest burden, or the burden of another, at the apex of the journey, on Monte Irago. Many recite the following prayer when leaving their rock at the Cruz de Ferro: *Lord, may this stone, a symbol of my efforts on the pilgrimage that I lay at the foot of the cross, weigh the balance in favor of my good deeds some day when the deeds of my life are judged. Let it be so.*

Because I knew of this tradition ahead of time, I had invested some forethought into the kind of rock I'd like to take to the cross. What was the biggest burden weighing me down in my life and keeping me from finding true happiness? It's not an easy question to answer, and in many cases it's that exact question that has propelled peregrinos onto the Camino in a quest for answers. This question is ageless and boundless; ill fitting for multiple choice or true/false, nor does this question just show up once in your life. Even if you answer it correctly, even if you have demonstrated mastery, you'll still have to answer it again and again.

Some pilgrims skip the pre-planning and just pick up a rock on the Camino to carry to the Cruz de Ferro. But like every lesson plan I ever created, I thought it through with painstaking preparation. I imagined every detail of the event so that it would be personal, meaningful, and symbolic of me and my journey. What kind of rock could I use? Should I find one in my backyard, or at the beach, or should I purchase one with extra meaning? What size, shape, color? A friend of mine is something of an expert on crystals, and she told me of a shop near her house that I could visit. Maybe I could see what they offered, and what "spoke to me." So I headed to this crystal shop, eager to discover a meaningful option.

Immediately when I entered, I realized I wouldn't have to conduct an arduous search for meaning. A very powerful energy greeted me in an instant, followed by a woman emerging from behind a curtain to offer assistance. I told her of my plans, and she made a few suggestions of stones to carry with me, both for protection and for healing. Then, she did something that absolutely amazed me. She pointed to a portrait on the wall of a girl about eight years old. She told me it was her daughter, Sarah, who had passed away a couple of years earlier. She told me that she had some rocks that her daughter had collected in life, and asked if I would take one to the cross and say a prayer.

I was overcome with awe and overwhelming honor. Of course, I would! She went back behind the curtain and returned with a box full of rocks— and something else that stunned me. Among all the rocks was a single shell. Just one shell, exactly like the shell that pilgrims carry on their journey on the Camino. The ultimate traditional symbol of the pilgrimage. When I commented on the shell, Sarah's mom said, "Oh, yeah, she collected all these rocks, but she also found this shell that she decided to keep too. She said it was special."

You could have knocked me over with a feather! I picked up the shell and told her about its symbolism on the Camino. We agreed that it was meant to be, and so, she entrusted it to me. I left the shop that day with a sense of gratitude and amazement, as well as a few rocks I purchased (the ones that had "spoken to me"). It was such a surreal feeling that I will never forget. When I look back on it now, it almost seems like a dream or an alternate universe. I have come to realize that when the Universe unfolds in miraculous and mysterious ways, the best choice is to "let go and let flow," because it is meant to be. It is part of a divine plan, and who am I to resist that?

As I approached the base of the cross, I pulled Sarah's shell from its special wrapping in my pack, feeling reverence for this moment finally arriving. I could see thousands of stones, notes, and pictures that had been left by other travelers. Words and names released from the hearts of those who had been suffering loss. Loss of others. Loss of self. There was a prayer card tacked to the cross that read: "You crossed my mind a time or two, and I asked the angels to be near you. I wished I could somehow be there. Even though I am not with you, know that you're in my heart and that I whispered a prayer or two for you."

With a lump in my throat, I placed the shell next to the prayer card and thought about Sarah's mom back home. I hoped that the pain and suffering from the loss of a child would be healed for her. I hoped that somehow peace and joy would return to her life. In that moment, I felt an enormous and overwhelming release of emotion, not only for Sarah and her mom, not only for all the names and prayers I could see before me, but also for myself and my inner child, in a myriad of ways. For my personal and professional self. For my younger self who had suffered several miscarriages, and hadn't known how to let go of the pain. For the innocence and wonder I'd sacrificed through the struggles and suffering of my life. I'd created a false inner child, my Ego, that had perpetuated a story of "bad," "not enough" and "not for you." I had turned to teaching to fill the hole in my heart, and my students had filled it with unconditional love and joy. All those years I taught, I had really been healing my own wounded inner child. I gave them everything that I didn't get as a child. I believed in their innocence and had faith in their spirit.

The stone I had chosen to leave was an Apache Stone of

Tears. I wanted to leave behind all of the tears of pain, sorrow, and regret that I had experienced from the many struggles in my life. I wanted my heart to be lighter and sing again. I wanted to set the intention that I would no longer choose to play the victim, but rather make the choice to know that life is unfolding for me exactly how it should, and that I should pause, reflect, and look for the lesson. Everything happens to teach me something about myself and the world around me, so WAKE UP, and stop hiding in fear. And, if I didn't get the main idea or essential understanding from the lesson the first time, then, try again. Life is not a test. Our experiences are for practice and growth, not for perfection and termination. The only real end to anything is death, so we feel and act as if our failures are death sentences. We allow failure to steal away hope. We especially allow others to do this—tell us "No, you can't," or "No, you won't," or "No, you shouldn't." No, no, no!

These messages are stop signs on the learning path, but not a place to pause for reflection. STOP trying. STOP believing. STOP hoping. **S** for STUPID. **T** for TERROR. **O** for OBSTACLES. **P** for PAIN. These are the words that keep us from moving forward: I am stupid. I am afraid. There are too many things standing in my way and keeping me from my dreams. I am hurting too much and just don't want to try. I just can't.

What if these stops were a place for reflection? **S** for SPIRIT, **T** for TRY again, **O** for OVERCOME, and **P** for PRACTICE and PRAISE.

I had the chance to witness this new kind of stop, at the Cruz de Ferro. The scene and energy there was amazing. Here, people were stopping to reflect on their journeys so far. All around me, they were praying, sobbing, peacefully releasing their stones at the base of the cross. You could almost see the stream of tears and sorrows rise up toward Heaven.

I didn't want to leave the cross. I felt so peaceful, and so much light. Many people seemed to feel the same way, as they gathered and stayed put, reading the many messages or taking in the faces in the pictures that were left at the cross. In a continuation of the tradition of leaving a stone, many people choose to pick up a stone that had been left behind, and carry it with them to symbolize that we help each other. This choice says that life is more like a relay race, and we each take turns carrying the burdens, making the sacrifices and suffering through the pain.

I understood the concept in theory, but I could not bring myself to actually do it, because I felt it was disrespectful, a bit like sacrilege. Someone had brought the stone to the cross with a personal and meaningful intention for them and the Divine. I didn't feel comfortable interfering with that unless I had a chance to talk to that person and find out more context, and even get permission to carry on with that intention. I'd had some of the same feelings in the classroom with regard to lesson plans. To me, lesson plans couldn't just be picked up and delivered impersonally without any connections or meaning. There is no magic lesson plan that will work miracles just like there is no magic purple pill that will cure everything that ails us, yet we complicate our lives and create added stress constantly seeking one singular "magic" solution.

The real magic, however, comes from inside. A stone may just be a stone, but each one left behind at the Cruz de Ferro was an embodiment of one human's unique story and struggles. They are a personal expression of each person's life and who you are. This kind of magic manifests from the soul and radiates like Divine light, inspiring awe and wonder in others to take the journey and seek understanding from their perspective as well.

Today, teachers seem to be only asked to hike up the hill of professional development to the iron cross of endless meetings to pick up the stones of others and carry them into the classroom. The latest strategy, the latest trend in pedagogy, the latest checklist of requirements to prove their worth as a teacher and the worth of their students. *Pick up all those stones and put them in your backpack, but don't bring any of yours to the cross.* To be a teacher worthy of "exceptional" or "exemplary" rating, you have to sacrifice yourself on the alter at the cross and pick up all those stones from others—or so we think. I believe that the "not enough" mentality plays out in the educational system to heartbreaking effect. It has become ingrained in the cells of every educator and student.

Everyone is carrying around stones and heavy backpacks that are weighing them down. We are taking on the stones of others and hanging on to our own that no longer serve a purpose or have meaning. We are just sacrificing ourselves to the legacy of martyrdom. We do more and more to be more and more and then we burn out. We buy in to the "work harder, not smarter" school of practice and check out of the "self-care" clinic.

We love teaching. We love learning. We love children. We feel a calling. We have a purpose. So, where are we going off path? Why are we so miserable in education today? Because we are coming to the cross and picking up the stones of others rather than being able to check in to our own hearts in order to bring our own gifts of wisdom and understandings to the cross. We have traveled the journey and crossed those obstacles. Let us share those greater understandings with children and guide them along their own personal path to their own greater understandings.

What the ritual at the cross truly does is allow for release and letting go in order to heal and move forward. It gives perspective on the piles of burdens that others also carry, each with its own story. We all have blisters, as Mary said. Instead of comparing them and setting standards for the number, size and degree of pain they cause, why are we not allowing for self-reflection, curiosity, and exploration of how they can teach me, or even relate to me?

As I stood at the base of the Cruz, I reflected on my journey so far, both on the Camino and in life. I had released some things from the past and got curious about the things that lie ahead of me. My mind wandered and explored the possibilities of a future free from the burdens I was leaving behind, albeit symbolically, at the Cruz de Ferro. That's all I could do. There were no guarantees, no foregone conclusions, no crystal ball. Just me and the next step. And somehow, that peace inside was enough in that moment.

16

Lessons learned

16.1 Personal Reflection Activity

Fill in this "iron cross" we all bear.

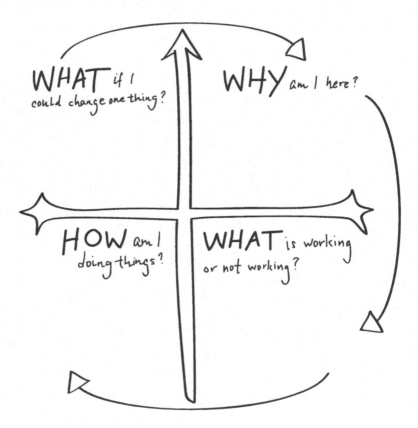

16.2 Interpersonal Connection Activity

Use the illustration of the Cruz de Santiago to start a conversation with someone that you are having a difficult relationship with at this time. Ask the other person the same questions and share your answers. Where are there still gaps or misunderstandings or roadblocks? Talk about the "what if's?" and how they would affect your relationship, for better or for worse.

17

FALLS, FAILURES AND F.E.A.R.

"The greatest glory in living lies not in never failing,
but in rising every time we fall."

—RALPH WALDO EMERSON, PHILOSOPHER

AFFIRMATION:

I may fall, but I do not fail as I get up, pause,
reflect and plan my next step forward

Eventually, I had to tear myself away from the scene at the Cruz de Ferro and keep going. I needed to start the descent into the next town where I would stay overnight. Buoyed by the experience at the cross, I set off with the expectation that the descent would be a piece of cake. The views were spectacular, and I felt as if I were walking on air. But soon, the path became very rocky and difficult to maneuver. It also became very easy to see how far the long path stretched ahead of me, and how much distance I still had to go.

Then, the perception that going downhill would be easy was shattered. It took so much more movement and energy to maneuver around the huge rocks on the path. The pads of the front of my feet were rubbing raw and my calves were beginning to burn from constantly using them to "brake" excessive forward motion of the descent. Other pilgrims were passing me, getting smaller and smaller in the distance that seemed to be getting longer and longer. And it was getting later and later. Worry began to nag at me. Would I be able to make it before it got dark?

Then, the landscape suddenly changed. It was charred black, a startling scene to stumble into. Evidently, there had been a fire on the side of the mountain, and the beauty of the landscape had disappeared. It was dismal and dark, echoing the shift in my mood from light and airy to heavy and dark. I was losing hope, even though I was going downhill. *It was supposed to be easier now. I had released my burdens. Why wasn't it working out according to the lesson plan? Why was I still not able to keep up with the others?*

My feet began bleeding, and the pain escalated to the point where I had to sit down. I looked around me at the charred landscape, feeling desperate and alone. I was resolved to die on the Camino, it seemed. The 87-year-old woman's words rang loud throughout my head.

"I'm so stupid."

"What was I thinking?"

"What's wrong with me?"

"I can't do this."

Then, I heard footsteps. Approaching me from further up the mountain was a man and his teenage son. The son was carrying a pack, but the father was just walking with sticks. They stopped and asked me, in Spanish, if I needed help. I told them that my feet were bleeding and that I didn't think I could make it. The father, Santiago, of all names, said that it wasn't that far, and that he would walk with me to make sure that I made it. He sent the son on to the village to wait for us and make sure that we did make it safely, telling him that if we didn't show up by nightfall to send the authorities out to find us.

It turned out that Santiago was actually *from* Santiago, too.

This struck my curiosity. Why would someone who lived in Santiago come all the way out here just to walk home? He said that he had come to walk the Camino with his family. I asked if he had more family walking than just his son. He explained that he did, but they had walked ahead because he was walking slowly. Only his son had stayed behind. My immediate first thought was one of judgment: *Hm. That doesn't seem much like spending time with family.*

Then, Santiago reached into my heart with his story, and I felt shame for my quick and harsh evaluation. He had found out that he had MS, and he didn't know how much more time he would be able to walk. He loved to spend time traveling with his family, so he came to the Camino to do just that. Being able to walk and being able to travel and be with his family. This was what was important to him and, therefore, this was what he put all his energy and attention on. He focused wholly on his intention, and everything else fell away.

Moved by his story, I shared with him that doctors had thought that I might have MS or ALS because of my difficulty walking, and told him how it had scared me into retirement. He said he, too, had retired for the same reason. But the difference was that he actually *had* MS, and was declining in health every day. Yet, here he was. He was managing the illness, and his expectations and outcomes for its effect on his life.

We got lost in our conversation, and I almost forgot about the pain, the blood, and the struggle. It was just one foot in front of the other, with a companion whose suffering put my own in perspective.

Eventually, we arrived at the village, greeted by his family, plus Jaime and Liliana, who waited with big smiles and open arms. Relief swept over us all, and after much thanking, we parted ways to find our respective hotels. I had planned to stay in a hotel that, inconveniently, turned out to share the same name as another hotel in the village. One was here at the beginning of the village, but the other was located at the other end of the village, about a half mile away.

I dearly hoped that I was staying at the one I was already standing in front of, but when I tried to check in, they said I must be staying at the other one. So, I started walking toward the other end of town. There were some other pilgrims walking the same route, looking as bewildered and confused as I was. Where was this hotel?

We got to the other end of town, which literally dead-ended in a cemetery. We all joked about how we hoped that wasn't our destination, given the way we were feeling in that moment, after the experience at the cross and the struggles of traversing the mountain. A small group now, we turned around and walked back to the first hotel, reporting that we couldn't find the other one. The staff there explained that we had to go *past* the cemetery, *around* the side of the hill, and *then* we would see it. So, we walked another half mile back (if you're keeping track, that's now a total of 1.5 extra miles), rounded the side of the hill, and there it was... high up on another hill. My feet seemed to scream in protest and frustration. I actually wanted to just scream out loud.

This "other" hotel was like a beacon on a hill. It was newly built, and quite spectacular, which made the day's final ascent even more surreal and anticipatory. Behind it was a huge pool that overlooked the mountains and valley below. The decorations were made from elements in nature to reflect the beauty of the countryside around it, reminiscent of the Spanish architect Antoní Gaudí. There was a serene and peaceful aura about it, for which I should have been incredibly grateful. After a day in which I felt as if I had fallen into the depths of Hell, this should have seemed like a little slice of Heaven on Earth.

Yet all my mind could do was replay the difficulties of the day, and review everything that had gone "wrong." The peaceful feeling I had at the Cruz de Ferro was like a distant memory, and in its place was a fog of negativity. I had forgotten the intense release of pain and suffering that I had there. I could not remember the lesson and enlightenment that I had gained there. I was not even spiraling into "woulda-coulda-shoulda" regretful thinking. Instead, my mind was reeling a new film of defeat, anger and resentment, which then manifested into everything I touched. My room was lovely, but it seemed as though I needed to use a shared bathroom facility down the hall. This would have been fine, except I looked for one and couldn't find it.

So I went to the front desk. While I stood there waiting for the young receptionist to acknowledge me, two young male pilgrims approached the desk. She immediately turned her attention to them, flirting with them as she offered answers and solutions. My patience for the whims of young romance was paper thin as I stood by and endured yet another obstacle in my quest to simply shower and take care of my bloodied aching feet. Finally, after what felt like an eternity, she turned to me, and, with a flippant attitude, asked what I wanted. I asked where the bathrooms were.

She rolled her eyes and said, "In your room, of course."

"In my room, where?"

"Behind the door by your bed, of course!" Another eye roll.

I hobbled back to my room and looked for a door beside the bed. Sure enough, there was a pocket door that had no handle and blended in with the wall. Was this a joke, an illusion or painful irony? Spaniards do enjoy irony in their literature and daily tales. Or like having two hotels with the same name in one small town, the path from one ending in a cemetery and the path to the other going uphill after a day of climbing to the highest point on the Camino. Seems like material for "Isn't It Ironic?" by Alanis Morrissette.

Eager to *finally* soak my raw and burning feet, I slid open the door... and was greeted with a shower stall only. I nearly screamed in anger.

"I can barely stand! Why the hell don't they have a bathtub? What kind of place is this?!" Somehow, in this hotel Eden with hidden bathrooms and boy-crazy receptionists, it was their fault that I was in so much pain.

By this point, my spirit was nearly as worn down as the skin on my feet. I took my boots off, and found that I had completely worn the skin off the pads of the front part of my feet, a result of the constant friction of walking downhill from the Cruz de Ferro. Wincing, I rinsed them thoroughly with the shower head, then decided just to go outside and soak them in the pool.

The cool water felt both painful and refreshing at the same time. It reminded me of my first day on the Camino, at Molino de Galochas, when I put my feet in the cold stream beside the inn. My mind and body had already been through so much since then, and yet, here I was, still struggling. I hadn't "perfected" things. Moreover, I was blaming everyone and everything outside of me for where I was now, in this moment. The mountains. The people in the past who had hurt me. The people who were shaming me. The people who didn't stay with me and support me or show sympathy. The guidebook had said the stage of the Camino today was supposed to be 16 kilometers and instead it was 26 kilometers.

Why the heck was I there? I had experienced the Camino, learned a few things, and now I was bruised and bleeding. Why not just go home? I imagined myself like an embattled soldier returning from war, bandages on their head and feet. I had suffered, I was wounded, I needed to heal.

I was ready to give up, again.

Then the Universe sent me exactly what I needed, again.

It was a small but significant fleet of hopeful reinforcements.

The first came when Jaime and Liliana showed up at my hotel and wanted to buy me a nice, fancy dinner. Not a basic pilgrims meal like I had been eating every day (or nothing at all some days). They encouraged me to "live in the present moment" and to believe in my ability to finish the Camino.

At dinner, Liliana shared stories of her early struggles on the Camino, suffering with blisters and losing toenails and not being able to walk. But each time she had survived, and has since chosen over and over to return to the Camino, because each time she grew as a human being in spirit. Our waitress saw my bandaged feet and encouraged me to keep going to Santiago, no matter what it took to get there, because it was worth it when you got to the cathedral and felt the grandeur of it all. The care from new friends and total strangers lifted me out of hopelessness.

When I finally laid my head on the pillow in the hotel on the hill, I felt more peaceful than when I'd arrived. Even so, I was still restless with nightmares. That word, *nightmare*, comes from the Old English "mare," a mythological demon or goblin who torments others with frightening dreams. That seems a little like an oxymoron, "frightening dreams." Dreams shouldn't be frightening. Dreams give us hope. Fear takes it away.

And that was what was happening. I was once again allowing fear to take away my hope of finishing the Camino. I was living in the fear of the future and the unknown. What if I had created permanent damage to my feet that would keep me from walking long distances ever again? If I left now, would I ever get a second chance to come back and finish? Moreover, what would people say and think when I returned home a failure? The bandages on my feet seemed to be emblazoned with a big, fat, bold letter L.

17

Lessons learned

17.1 Personal Reflection Activity

Revolver in Spanish means to "return again," as in: you have another chance in the circle of learning.

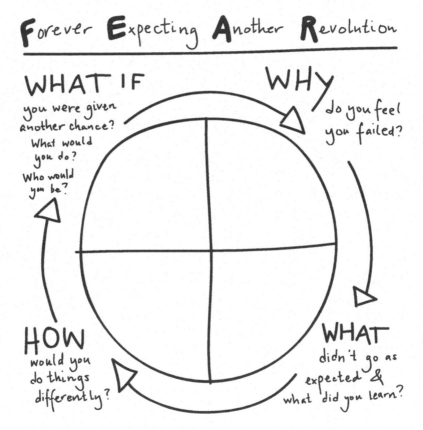

Forever Expecting Another Revolution

WHAT IF
you were given
another chance?
What would
you do?
Who would
you be?

WHY
do you feel
you failed?

HOW
would you
do things
differently?

WHAT
didn't go as
expected &
what did you learn?

17.2 Interpersonal Connection Activity

Ask someone you admire to tell you a story about some fear that they had struggled with in their life over and over again, and how they eventually overcame it. As they are telling their story, keep in mind the graphic from the Personal Reflection activity and see how much or how little their story follows the "revolution."

18

LIFTED UP ON THE WINGS OF ANGELS

"Try to be a rainbow in someone else's cloud."
—MAYA ANGELOU, POET & AUTHOR

AFFIRMATION:

I have a little guardian angel that sits on my shoulder and whispers all the wisdom I need to make my heart flutter and fly like the wings of a bee flitting from flower to flower to sip the sweet nectar within.

I got up at dawn to meet Jaime and Liliana, who had made the mini-trek up the hill to greet me outside of my hotel. Although the bleeding had stopped, I would not be walking anywhere today. So I said goodbye to them for now, as they continued on their way, feet and spirits much more intact than my own. I watched them for quite a while as they walked downhill, getting smaller and smaller in my view. I was alone with my aching body and churning mind, forced to take at least a day to recover. Now what?

I tried to turn my attention to the beautiful view of the mountains and valley surrounding the hotel. Being in Mother Nature had always been a calming and grounding force for my spirit, but yesterday it felt as if she had turned on me. Too many rocks, too much altitude, too much distance, too many charred, desolate, and depressing hillsides. Too much this, too much that. *How could she betray me and then abandon me like this?* My monkey mind immediately turned to the people in my life that I had felt had done the same.

Thankfully, the ugly voices in my head were interrupted by a voice asking me, in Spanish, how I was. I looked up to see a young woman cleaning and tidying the lobby area. I responded in Spanish, and upon realizing I could communicate with her in her native language, she introduced herself. Her name was Sandra, and she was from Nicaragua. She told me that she had just finished walking the Camino last week and that she had returned to this place because she "had a feeling" that called her back here. She loved talking to the pilgrims and hearing their stories and sharing her story with them. She felt that there was an exchange of hope among the pilgrims, and that the currency was stories. So, she told me hers.

Sandra had a very rough life in Nicaragua, and needed to get away from abuse and dangerous situations with drug lords. It is not uncommon, unfortunately, for Indigenous women in Central American countries to become enslaved by drug lords at innocent and vulnerable ages, between 10-12 years old. In Sandra's case, friends and even strangers had given her money and supplies to be able to fly to Spain and walk the Camino. She told me that faith, and trust, and a sense of belief from others helped carry her on the Camino. She showed me pictures of her journey and shared stories of some of the others she had met along the way, and from whom she had learned so much.

The "feeling" that called her back was a feeling of giving back what she had received—the spirit of love, generosity, kindness, support, trust, faith, and hope. She was doing that for me, and I was humbled to be a part of this chain of humanity that defined her life. As we chatted and got to know each other, she kept giving me hugs and offering words of reassurance. Finally, before we parted ways, she said something that I will NEVER forget: "You are a true lucera on the Camino, and that is what will carry you through to Santiago."

"Lucera" comes from the word "luz" in Spanish, which means "light." There are so many connections for that meaning: light as in "lighting the way for others," like in teaching. Light like in "dar a luz" which literally means "to give light," but is used to mean "to give birth." Through our journeys of learning, we are giving birth to new ideas, perspectives and experiences that help us grow as human beings. They light the way for us moving forward toward our True Selves.

For Sandra, she said a "lucera" is "one who gives light and vision to others," and that is why I was a teacher. It was my God-given gift that I needed to share with the world. It was my calling, and it gave me a fulfilling career nurturing all kinds of learners, young and old. But she also said that giving light was my gift as a healer to those I met casually in life, or to my family and friends. These words shook me from the "victim" mode that had been darkening my thoughts since I started the Camino. Yes, I had needed help from kind strangers like Santiago, and Mary, and Liliana. But I was also in a position to give help to others who needed it. I had witnessed so much generosity and benevolence already along the Camino, but I had been too immersed in my own fear to realize that my role was not simply one of helplessness. My strengths as an educator remained strengths here, on this seemingly different path: even though I was not "in the classroom," I could give light to others, and carry on the legacy of helping and nurturing those in need.

It was at that moment that I vowed to become more aware of how my Ego and my own suffering were occupying my attention. There's a kind of spiritual paradox that I hadn't really grasped until this moment. We think that if we look outside of ourselves for answers, we'll never find the true knowledge we seek. But often, when we're lost and off path, the way back to our True Selves is illuminated when we shine a light for someone else. As I shifted my perception so that "teacher" and "healer" were sourced from the same gifts, I vowed to spend the rest of the Camino listening to others and their stories, because as I listened to them, I was not only healing myself, I was healing them in spirit.

There are a million ways of saying it, but basically: what we give, we receive. Service in spirit is the highest purpose in life, and it had been my highest purpose as a teacher. Thanks to Sandra, I was reminded of that belief from which I had somehow lost my way. Now I was going to focus on it like I had in the classroom, and light the way ahead, for myself and others. It had served me well then, and I knew it would work its magic again here on the Camino.

•   •   •

As Sandra's profound wisdom sank deep into my soul, I fell into a state of calm reverie. My own path through life had been lit by luceras, and rerouted by obstacles, like anyone's. As I grew into adulthood and made choices about my future, I found that I have certain things that I am good at. I also discovered things I am not so good at. We all go through this, especially in our youth.

When we're kids, we get input from other people about what our talents and shortcomings are. For instance, I was told I was good at math, so in 9th grade, I thought I might like to have a career involving math skills. This carried forward to the point of getting certified to teach math, since it was a requirement to teach at the old high school I had graduated from. But, ultimately, I found that communicating through numbers and formulas did not inspire me.

I had also been told I had a good ear for music, so I started taking piano lessons. I had musical aunts and uncles, and it seemed a logical inheritance. So I got a job as a "soda jerk" in a local pharmacy in order to pay for piano lessons. (When I told this story to my students, I had to explain how pharmacies used to have a "soda fountain" and also offer ice cream. These went the way of the Dodo not long after I worked at one.) I continued pursuing music through high school, with good results. However, when I auditioned for the music program at a prestigious music school in Florida, I was told that I was "good," but that I had not been playing long enough to develop the skills they were looking for. Apparently they only took students who had started taking piano at a very young age...probably as soon as they came out of the womb!

Knocked down by this kind of elite exclusivity in education, I had to reevaluate my future plans. I was devastated by the rejection, I felt like a "failure"...lost, confused and not knowing which way to turn. I had thought that music was my calling and my gift. But it turns out that wasn't true, and the Universe steered me in another direction.

Instead of the prestigious music school, I ended up at my local community college, where I completed one year of coursework before transferring to my local university. Like so many incoming freshmen, I didn't have a strong idea about my major yet. I was still examining the things I loved and trying to figure out a way to incorporate them into a career path. I was studying French and Spanish, but wasn't quite sure yet the best way to mobilize those skills. My French teacher, Madame Carrell, also served as my college advisor, and quickly scheduled a formal appointment to meet with me and go over my future plans.

As it happened, the weekend before my Monday morning appointment, I flew on an airplane for the first time. I was headed to New York City to attend something called "Acceptance Day" at the United States Merchant Marine Academy, where my then-boyfriend, now-husband, had just entered as a cadet. "Acceptance Day" took place at the end of the first month of attendance, and sounded like an amazing celebration. But really it was a commemoration of survival: the first month required physical and mental regulation, "to develop character and discipline." This educational approach was designed to build resilience, but there were so many standardized conditions and rules that most cadets struggled to feel accepted and like they were "enough" throughout their four years.

Acceptance Day aside, I decided to visit the United Nations while I was in the Big Apple. I wanted to find out what it would take to become an interpreter there, since I loved Spanish and French. Like the music college, they basically turned their noses up and said that they only hired native speakers. Once again, I felt completely heartbroken about these dashed dreams, and the Universe redirected me again... this time to Jackson, Mississippi.

On my return flight, I did my best to manage my disappointment and prepare myself for the college advisor appointment with Madame Carrell. Sitting primly in my brand new powder blue pantsuit (every corner of this story is Very 70s), I went through a mental roster of my passions. Languages... the humanities... the arts... travel? I would love to see the world. Maybe I could talk to Madame Carrell about becoming a stewardess, as they were called then. I watched one of the stewardesses pass me by, carrying a tray of beverages, and felt a twinge of doubt. In those days, there were age, height, and weight requirements that I surely would not meet.

Come to find out, I would have been a miserable stewardess, because my ears plug up terribly when I fly. As the plane landed in Atlanta, my stopover, I couldn't hear the announcement of gate numbers for any connecting flight, let alone my connection to Jacksonville. So, with muffled ears, I asked a stewardess which gate I needed. She asked, kindly, to see my ticket. I feebly waved it at her like a flash card. She got a fleeting look at it and pointed me to a gate nearby, where people were already in line and boarding.

So, I hurried over to the line, and waved the same boarding

pass at the attendant at this gate. Phew! Airport navigation successful. Jacksonville, here I come!

The flight was very short, but also bumpy, which put me on edge. I thought the worst of it came when we hit a big bump, and a stewardess went flying across the aisle... and helplessly tipped her tray of drinks directly onto my lap. My brand new pantsuit was now stained to the point that I looked like a wet, sticky Dalmatian. I tried to sop up all the liquid on my clothing, and then... we began our descent to land.

Puzzled, I craned my neck to see out the window. *That was an awfully short flight.* We sank lower and lower, and the airport swam into view. *...that doesn't look like the terminal at the Jacksonville Airport.*

Well, that's because it wasn't. I was landing in Jackson, Mississippi. Apparently, my hand had covered the "ville" in Jacksonville when I showed the attendants my ticket, and as (bad) luck would have it, there was a flight nearby that just happened to be going to Jackson...no *ville*!

The next flight out was not until 7:00 the next morning, so I spent the night crying (and crying) in the airport bathroom. I tried desperately to wash the stains out of my pantsuit, because now I would have to go straight from the airport to my college advisor appointment with Madame Carrell the next morning. What would I do now? *I can't be a stewardess if my ears plug up and I can't hear anything! And I can't convince Madame Carrell of my bright future when I can't even get on the right plane!*

Fortunately, the Universe once again stepped in and sent me an angel. It turned out to be the cleaning lady. This poor woman did her best to console me when she found me sobbing in the bathroom. Not only that, when I explained how lost I was (and not just geographically), she tried to help me figure out what to do. She asked questions about who I was, where I was from, what

I loved, what my hopes and dreams were, what I was good at, what was my favorite subject in school. I told her about school, my favorite subjects and, of course, stories about my teachers and the impact they all had on me, both good and bad.

I ended up following her around all night, telling her story after story. She listened patiently and intently, as if I were her favorite music channel on the radio. Looking back, I realize now that this woman was a lucera. Sure, no one takes a pilgrimage to the Jackson Airport, but I was on a journey where a kind stranger guided me when I was wayward and powerless. It was such a magnificent lesson on the power that each and every one of us has to be a teacher-guide-mentor and to make a difference in the life of another human being, especially a young person. That was my *aha!* moment, right in the middle of one of the worst *oh no* experiences I'd had so far in my young life.

The next morning, I bid farewell to my lucera, and boarded the first flight out of Mississippi, finally on my way home. I made it to my appointment with Madame Carrell, who graciously ignored my disheveled appearance. Soon thereafter, the way ahead finally illuminated, I started on my path as a teacher.

But more importantly, I continued on my path as a lifelong learner. What I have come to realize is that we are all teachers and learners on this journey called life. Like Sandra had said, we each bring a special gift into the world to share with others. I chose to answer the calling to become a teacher in the classroom, but the greater lessons in life certainly came outside of the classroom.

18

Lessons learned

18.1 Personal Reflection Activity

Think about what kind and generous actions resonate in your heart and fill in the chart below with at least one example per bubble.

18.2 Interpersonal Connection Activity

At the beginning of each day, set an intention to be a "lucera" (or a lucero, the masculine version) in someone else's day. What random act of kindness or words of encouragement and inspiration can you gift to that person? At the end of the day, fill out the other part of the illustration with how you think you helped light the way for that person and how it made you feel.

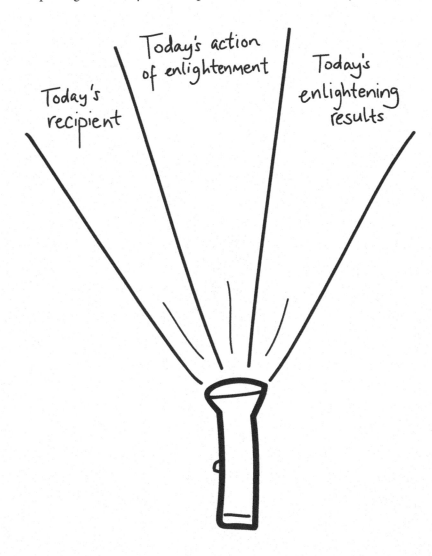

19

FINDING THE SHATTERED PIECES OF OURSELVES

"When you see yourself in a shattered mirror, don't think of it as the broken pieces of yourself, think of it as all the pieces that make you up."

—BLAQUE DIAMOND, AUTHOR

AFFIRMATION:

I pick up the broken and shattered pieces of my heart so that they might be put back together by the love I have inside me that is always the true glue that holds me together.

Heartened by Sandra's words, I now had a renewed commitment to be a lucera of service to those around me, just as I was as a teacher in the classroom. And who did the Universe send me in order to test this commitment, but a young person— not quite a high school student, but a young man in his early 20s. Victor was working at the hotel for the summer to earn money to buy a race car. He loved cars and wanted to come to the States to become a race car driver. His family wanted him to go to college, but he said that wasn't what he felt in his heart. Naturally, I asked him about school, and he said he didn't like it at all. It was too much "from the book" and not enough "real life." He said that students had to do and be the same, which didn't resonate with him. He was bored. After learning that I was a Spanish teacher, he talked a lot about his experience learning English and how he hated it. There was no room for creativity, individuality or following one's own passion or interests, like race cars. It was all prescribed medicine, and he didn't need the "cure." He was fine. The teacher barely knew English and just made them memorize things from the book and listen to recordings and repeat everything. Well, that sounded familiar! He said he learned more English from YouTube and from talking to tourists at the hotel. It was only through these methods that he discovered that he really did like learning English, especially when it enabled him to talk with other people, learn about them, and share about himself.

Isn't this the purpose of communication? To build relationships and learn from each other? To make connections and build community? It's so simple, yet we make it so complicated. When we're first learning a language, we choose words from the vocabulary we know. Straightforward. No other intention than to communicate a need or desire. Very little interpretation is needed on the part of the other person.

But as we grow our language skills and our vocabulary base, boy oh boy, how we complicate our communication! Inference, hidden intentions, and emotional overtones break up (and break down) the lines of communication. We don't really say what we mean, nor do we really mean what we say. I truly love the quote by Mahatma Gandhi about happiness: "Happiness is when what you think, what you say and what you do are in harmony." That is the truest definition of happiness I know. It's so simple, but so hard to achieve. So much gets in the way of the communication between our hearts and our heads, and then, what comes out of our mouths may even be something else entirely. We lose our truth in translation and the interpersonal exchange that ensues becomes a ping pong match of misinformation and deceptions, intentional or subconscious. Either way, it usually leads to hurt.

Wouldn't it be great if our school classes focused more on learning how to effectively—and kindly—express our true thoughts and feelings? This is the communication skill we really need: the ability to build bridges of connection. Without these tools of self-expression, we find ourselves on a vast battlefield of landmines and pitfalls that threaten to devastate our relationships—both with ourselves and with others. I am filled with hope to see that more and more schools are incorporating mindfulness into their school culture. To practice mindfulness is to become more aware of your thoughts, feelings and physical sensations in order to monitor, regulate, and communicate them more effectively to others. Again, it sounds simple, but like any new learning, it needs to be experienced and practiced in order to build the skills.

Talking with Victor led me to revisit a question teachers are always called to reflect on: are schools actually equipping young learners with what they will need in life? Yes, "soft skills," like communication, stress management, and adaptability are being overlooked—but what about the "hard skills," too? Are we even offering subject areas that students really want to learn?

In the United States, we have almost completely eliminated classes that allow students the opportunity to explore and develop skills for a trade. We used to have vocational education that taught auto mechanics, hairdressing, and business skills. Students would have on-the-job internships and training as a part of a school-to-work program. But today, every child is expected to go to college—and to *want* to go to college. Students like Victor don't fit into that school system, and face challenges with conforming, just as he described to me. For a college-driven school system, the ultimate goal is to seek a degree in the latest most profitable industry, that will assure them the most "success" in life. A degree that will earn them more money and more status.

Yet I had many students who just wanted to earn a living by fishing (in case you ever needed confirmation that I did, indeed, teach in Florida). They loved being on a boat, and just wanted to build a career around fishing and boats: charter fishing for tourists, shrimping to earn money, or even just bringing in the day's catch to the docks and selling to locals who wanted fresh fish for dinner. Despite the fact that "filleting a fish" is not a "valuable" skill recognized by formal education, it's still a skill. For some, it's even an art form!

Students like these don't necessarily need to go to college in order to have a successful future. Nor should they have to seek validation that they are "contributing to society" by the narrow standards of "success." Where is that message in school? "You don't have to go to college. Maybe you can go to a trade school." Why shouldn't school counselors provide more information about vocational careers, and offer meaningful guidance to support kids like that? School counselors, like teachers, spend so much time juggling the "stakeholders" to which they are accountable—students, parents, teachers, administrators, district and state personnel. They're constantly building, maintaining, and re-building those bridges of communication just to keep the peace among all those factions. Most of them have too many students, and too much paperwork, especially surrounding test scores and checklists. This leaves them too little time to get to the heart of what matters most to the real "customers": the students.

Soon after I returned home from the Camino, I had a chance to spend time at a school called Ak'Tenamit in the jungles of Guatemala. It was started by an American who had dropped out of high school because he was bored and saw no connection between what he was learning and the "real world." When he started his own landscape business in Florida, it turns out most of the men he hired were from Guatemala. As he got to know them better, he was curious as to why they had left everything behind that they called "home" to come to this new and strange country to start a new life. So, he went to Guatemala and discovered the poverty and danger in which these workers once had to live. He was horrified by the treatment of the Indigenous people, especially the young girls who were sold and/or captured into slavery at 10-12 years old. They couldn't go to school or become educated in any way to become free. Seeing a way to be of service, the man stayed and established Ak'Tenamit to give an education to these young girls.

What started with a few girls now has grown into a school for boys and girls both, with an enrollment of 500 students. They live in the jungle with no modern amenities like running water and electricity. Every student is part of the community that sustains their existence and their education. The school focus is to build community and meet the needs of the local community. So, the students have two tracks that they choose from: tourism or environmental sustainability. For tourism, students can learn hospitality management, how to be a chef, how to develop NGO and Fair Trade goods to market and sell. For environmental sustainability, they learn how to take care of the environment, how to grow food more effectively, how to market and sell what they grow. At the end of the 12th grade, the school gets every student an internship and on-the-job training. After the internship, they help get the students jobs in businesses like restaurants and guiding on eco-tours for the tourists who come to Belize nearby.

The education at Ak'Tenamit is designed to meet the needs of the individual students and communities. Moreover, it cultivates the values of giving back. Students often return to their local villages and give back with their education in order to make it a better place for all: with fair trade goods, increased quantity and quality of food crops, better infrastructure to the village. In doing so, they become role models and hope for the young children and their families who are there. Older students at Ak'Tenamit mentor and counsel younger students who might be struggling developmentally. Students who have graduated come back to be on the Board and run the school. Students have sponsors who pay $1 per day for tuition, room and board. If students can't pay or don't have a sponsor, their parents can pay with corn or beans equivalent to $1 per day—or less, considering inflation.

The school operates on a low budget, but mostly it operates on the human spirit of love, kindness, compassion, empathy, generosity, gratitude, community and joy. It radiates what is true school spirit. They have no sports team through which to channel and define this spirit. They don't wear special jerseys or don themed colors on Fridays. There is no spirit week of pajama day, twin day or superhero day. The essence of education and its place in their world is what drives everyone. It is awe-inspiring and truly touches the hearts of all who visit to see it in action. I wish this kind of true school spirit for all students and teachers in education.

•　　•　　•

It took me three days of shameful taxi rides before I was healed up enough to walk again. As much as I tried to let go of my "failure," I just tortured myself mentally to make up for the brief respite from physical wear. Each morning, I would wave goodbye to Jaime and Liliana, who set out with their packs on foot. Then, I would return to my room and spend some time soaking my feet in salt water, a painful but ultimately helpful practice. As I winced at the touch of biting water to my raw skin, I tried to appreciate the small success in having finally discovered what worked best to heal my feet.

But, truthfully, success seemed unavailable to me. My frustration was high and my feelings of hope were low. I had learned so many lessons and had so many epiphanies since I first started the Camino. I had made so many recommitments to purpose, and yet, here I was, in this state again. My body bruised. My thoughts a swirl of negative self-talk.

I had plenty of time to sit with myself and interrogate these feelings, even if the cab rides were much shorter than a whole day of walking. Why hadn't I mastered this yet? Why hadn't I *learned*?

This thought hit me like a ton of bricks. It was as if I was standing in front of Señorita Ortiz's desk again, completely assured that because I had passed all my Spanish I tests, I was perfectly equipped for Spanish II. When I was young, I thought that learning was linear. It was a checklist, right? You go in a sequential order, and once something is checked, you move forward, never to return. You take a course, you read a book, you acquire the knowledge, and then you're proficient. Right?

But of course, when I became a teacher, I knew better. And here I was, learning this lesson again—an irony in and of itself. We expect that once we "learn" something, i.e. pass the test and get a good grade, that means we have mastered it. Not just in a classroom, but in our own lives. When we touch a hot stove, we remember to never do it again, right? If only it were that simple.

"Practice makes perfect" is a deceptive little maxim. It almost encapsulates the right idea, in that it emphasizes the importance of practice in a learning journey. But "perfection" is a mirage on the horizon, a glittering fountain in the desert that is always, ALWAYS, a dusty boulder in disguise. Perfect is not the goal, because it's an impermanent illusion.

Practice makes me better, but never perfect. Keep the expectations real and manageable. I have found that one of the most difficult things for me to manage in my life is expectations, both those I set on myself and those placed upon me from others, which at this point are one in the same. "How long is it going to take me to get this through my head?" is an FAQ on the website of my life. The answer is always, "As long as it takes," which more realistically should be "your whole life." I have since adopted the mantra, "Learning isn't over until breathing has stopped!" So, no matter what, it's all good.

In Spanish, there's actually an adage that fits the mantra well: "No hay mal de que lo bien venga." "There is no bad that good doesn't come from." Some equate it to "Every cloud has its silver lining." Another great adage is "No hay mal que dure cien años, ni cuerpo que lo resiste." Loosely translated: "Nothing is forever." With every breath we take and every step we take, we are learning how to be in spirit, to be more present in this world and of this world before we leave this world, forever. It's an ongoing process. Keep going and growing.

Leaving the village behind me, I started walking again on a flat stretch—but the path was going to start climbing again. While it wouldn't go as high as the Cruz de Ferro, guidebooks and videos had indicated that it was the rockiest and steepest part yet, and a difficult climb. It didn't take long before frustration set in because I was going even slower than ever. Each step was painful and carefully taken so as to not damage my feet more. So, Jaime and Liliana went on ahead, and I painfully took one slow step after another.

After a couple of hours, a lady came racing by me. She was like a gazelle on the Camino. She said hello, and then veered off into the woods to pee. A few minutes later (only a few steps for me), she emerged on the path, stopped and introduced herself. She said that she noticed I was struggling with walking and asked if she could walk with me for a while. I welcomed the company of a new face and story. Christy was from California and in her 40s. She talked about her many failed relationships, which seemed she was almost literally running away from. Like me, she had been afraid to be alone on the Camino, and so she attached herself to a 27-year-old German boy named David in St. Jean Pied-de-Port. She was wealthy and had paid his hotel, meals and bought him clothes, shoes and even a bicycle. Yes, a bicycle! David had asthma and was going to quit the Camino, but Christy bought him the bicycle so that he could still escort her on the Camino and not induce an asthma attack. But David was nowhere to be seen, now. He had gone ahead, despite her gifts.

As I listened to her story, I thought about a quote by Marianne Williamson that says we are either running toward or away from love (same with fear). Christy seemed to be doing both. She was afraid of being alone, of being abandoned, of being helpless. I have that same fear. I think we all do. I remember one particular Oprah show that had an impact on me related to this. The guest psychologist asked audience members questions about difficulties in relationships with family, friends and partners. What he demonstrated was that after peeling back the many layers (humans are like ogres are like onions, after all), the core of their challenges was a feeling of abandonment.

As humans, we are wired for connection, which drives our need for love, acceptance and belonging, but it also drives our fear of abandonment, our fear of not being enough, our fear of being helpless. This fuels our need for permission and approval: we want to be ourselves and do what truly is in our hearts, but only if it meets the approval and expectations of others, so that we're not rejected, abandoned or helpless.

At first, I'd been taken aback that someone as fast as Christy would want to walk with me and my inchworm pace. I told her she didn't need to stay behind with me and walk so slowly. I thought I was holding her back. But then, I realized that by walking with me, she was somehow giving herself "permission" to slow down and not push herself so much. She mentioned many times how grateful she was to walk with me and not go so fast. She said she was happy to stop and enjoy the little things along the Camino, like taking pictures and getting a cold drink or snack. She had been going so fast to cover the required ground that she wasn't stopping to enjoy the experience. She had been pushing herself so hard that she was absolutely exhausted and running on adrenaline, which made her anxious and nervous.

She reminded me of myself when I was teaching. Most teachers are pushing themselves every day in the classroom to the point of adrenal burnout. People outside of the profession constantly talk about how teachers have summers off, and so many other holidays during the year...capped with a snarky "Must be nice!"

The truth is that there is no "off" in teaching. At night and on weekends, we are grading papers and preparing lesson plans. During holiday breaks, we are grading papers and preparing lesson plans in between the family festivities. During the summer, we are taking or giving professional development courses in order to renew our teaching certificates, which will allow us to work another five years for the same pay (or less, considering inflation and increase in the cost of living). Burnout is prevalent and predictable, yet we are not changing anything to prevent it. Why is that?

Christy was grateful to have someone listen who didn't want something in return. The fact is, meeting her and hearing her story, she had already given me so much in return, and she didn't even realize it! I received the gifts of her affirmations and lessons about managing expectations, running away from—or to—something and practicing self-care, self-love and self-acceptance. The true wealth of the soul is not found in dollars but in the currency of spirit. As I was becoming more open and vulnerable, I was also fulfilling my purpose as a "lucera," just as Sandra had said. I was not only there to learn, I was also there to walk with others and light the way toward a common vision of discovering the answer to the most essential questions of life: "Who am I? Why am I here?"

19

Lessons learned

19.1 Personal Reflection Activity

On a piece of paper, make a list of 5 positive memories you have and then, a list of 5 negative memories you have. Next to each memory, write an emotion associated with that memory. Don't use the same emotion more than once!

POSITIVE EMOTION	POSITIVE MEMORY	NEGATIVE EMOTION	NEGATIVE MEMORY

19.2 Interpersonal Connection Activity

Give a blank copy of the chart from the Personal Reflection Activity to someone you know well and ask them to fill it out as you did and cut into pieces. In one pile, both of you place the cards with the memories on them. In another pile, both of you place the cards with the emotions on them.

Then, taking turns, choose a card from the memory pile and one card from the emotion pile and see if they match. This will quickly turn into a "perception" discussion as the other person may not see how a certain emotion might be associated with the memory chosen.

Discuss this by sharing perspectives and stories to learn from each other as well as to become more aware of the emotions we are attaching to certain memories.

20

GENEROSITY OF THE HEART

*"A generous heart, kind speech and a life of service
and compassion are the things that renew humanity."*

—BUDDHA

AFFIRMATION:

*I give generously of myself from the heart so that I might be
the piece that makes peace in the heart of another.*

By the time I had walked two weeks on the Camino, I hadn't talked to my family once. Looking back, it's easy to see how being disconnected from them made my early experiences all the more challenging. So, finally, we made arrangements to talk by Skype, coincidentally at a time when they were visiting North Carolina. They had traveled by car, and it struck me that they had covered 400 miles in an eight-hour trip, whereas I was covering about 15 in the same time span on foot.

Planes, trains, and automobiles really have changed the human experience. With the interstate, we get in the car and get to our destination as fast as we can. There's very little to look at and enjoy along the way. Few stops and few pleasures to remember. And it can be stressful, with cars racing past you, weaving in and out of traffic, or riding your bumper so closely that you can't even see their headlights. This is such an embodiment of so many teachers' daily existence in the classroom today. No wonder teachers are so stressed and suffer with anxiety that then spirals into "road rage." They are too often in fight-or-flight mode, urging our "cars" to go faster and faster as if we were Jeff Goldblum in Jurassic Park.

Teachers feel such an intense pressure to teach more, cover more content, and keep up the pace. The lesson plan is always more, more, more, and stay on target. Don't fall behind or you will never get ahead...in life! The stakes feel enormous and the pace breakneck. As a result, we may cover more ground in the curriculum, but like the experience on the interstate, how much is really taken in, enjoyed, and remembered? There is no motivation or reason to take detours or make stops because the real goal is to get there as fast as we can.

What a shame it is. Learning should be soul-filling. It should be "about the journey, and not the destination," so the saying goes.

Of course, on the Camino, the journey was consuming my days, and the destination seemed more and more achievable with every step I took. As I walked further, I got better at staying in the present moment. I was learning to enjoy everything around me: the beauty of the countryside, the beauty of the people whom I was meeting.

Walking through the next town, I felt an urge to turn down a side street—to go off path. As I meandered down the lane, I saw a sign with a green cross on it, which is the symbol of a pharmacy in Spain. Inspiration struck: while I am here in the city, I should get some more supplies for my feet! As I approached the pharmacy, something else caught my attention. A man around 40 years old was waving at me from inside the neighboring storefront. He was surrounded by displays of shoes. *Aha!* I thought. Maybe I could buy new shoes that didn't rub my feet so much. Why on earth hadn't I thought of that sooner?

Hopeful for more successful solutions to my foot pain, I went inside, much to the waving man's delight. He spoke to me first in Spanish, then in French. When I replied in both languages, he seemed confused and even a little agitated. He followed this by rapidly telling me everything about his family and their business and the shoes they sold. I knew immediately that he likely had an autism spectrum disorder. I had worked with enough students through the years to recognize its characteristics, no matter what language they spoke.

Then, two people in their 70s emerged from behind the rows of shoes and greeted me. These were his parents, and they spoke to him gently and kindly, directing him to allow them a minute to ask me a few questions. I introduced myself and explained the troubles that I had been having on the Camino with my feet. They assured me it was normal, and then asked their son, José Manuel, what he would suggest for me. He enthusiastically hurried to a row of shoes in the back of the store and returned with a pair of sandals cupped in his hands. With an eager smile on his face, he held them out like a blessed offering or a heartfelt gift.

"Try them on," he said.

As I took the sandals from him, his father continued guiding the interaction. "What about socks?"

José Manuel hurried away again, this time to another aisle in the store. He returned with a pair of high heat intensity socks (not wool!) that would produce less friction and wick away any moisture to keep the foot from sliding and causing blisters. The sandals would allow my feet to breathe, even with the socks, and there would not be any heat from friction. Genius!

Before I had left for the Camino and as I was gathering all my survival supplies and "perfect/necessary" equipment, I had been told that I would need support and protection for my feet, and therefore, hiking boots were the best option. Waterproof, high-top hiking boots one half size bigger than my foot, to allow for swelling and sliding. It was sound in theory, but wasn't José's approach just as valid? And I loved that his parents just asked questions and helped him find the way to help me!

There are so many choices and options for the "shoes" we'll wear as we walk through life. As with any choice, we need to try some on, walk a little, and figure out if they are the best fit for us. If they cause blisters, then we need to find another pair that will better fit our feet and where we are walking.

I realized, socks and sandals in hand, that my shoes had become a kind of metaphor for making choices in life. I was intent on following the guidance of expert advice, and even though I wasn't experiencing success, I didn't even consider that I could pursue a better option until I wandered in front of this shoe store by happenstance. My first pair of shoes didn't serve my purpose or fit my needs, and I simply needed to change them and try again. No pair of shoes is for a lifetime. We can change our shoes whenever we want. What becomes confusing is when we have a closet full of shoes, and we are not sure where we are going or what the path might be like. We have to have options, but we also need to pick the right shoes for the occasion, for our path, and for what will support our own feet best.

To be honest, the anticipated ridicule of wearing socks with sandals briefly flashed through my mind, but I dismissed it easily for comfort and hope. I told José that I would take the sandals and the socks…two pair of socks, in fact! After I had finished paying, the father said that his name was also José, José Francisco, and asked if I wanted to see something. My first inkling was to say no. "I have to go, because I am already behind schedule today and I need to get to my next destination. I walk so slowly, you know!"

But instead, I nodded and said, "Sí." It turned out there was a lot to see… and hear! What unfolded in the next hour with the Blanco family was something I will never forget.

First, José Francisco showed me with great pride and expertise the 100-year-old equipment that his father used to start the business a century ago, and how they still use it for making and repairing shoes today. The shop was filled with family photos and treasured heirlooms. He showed me his rock collection, and pictures of him proudly posing on top of various mountains. He had been an alpinist, and rather athletic in his youth, he told me. His enthusiasm lulled for a contemplative moment, but then, he moved on to pictures of his childhood. Both he and his wife, Ofelia, told me stories about where they were born, how they met, and how they had learned to make shoes and help people with any foot-related issues. After all, they shared with a smile, feet were what carried us through life, and their location on the Camino positioned them where people arguably needed them most.

This perspective gave them such pride and purpose in their work. They lovingly talked of how they had passed that knowledge down to their son, José Manuel, and how he would carry on this family purpose and share his gifts with others on their paths. They mentioned that it took him a while to learn things, and that they still had to guide him on his path because of that. "But after all," José Francisco shrugged, "That is our duty and purpose as parents, right? It is also our duty as elders to guide the young and show them the way. We have mastered many things in our many years here on this earth, and we can be of use to help guide the young. However, there is still always so much to learn and share with others."

My heart and spirit were making so many connections to what he was saying—as a teacher, as a parent, as a human being. I felt the energy of their hearts: light and full of love and joy. They never dwelled on negative things in our conversation, like how they made it through the Franco era in Spain, or any challenges in raising José Manuel, or how their business was now further off the Camino than it had been in days gone by, and therefore, further from customers to help and money to keep the business alive.

They were quixotic and open-hearted in spirit, and welcomed others to share in that love and joy of their lives.

Time seemed to stand still while I was there, completely immersed in so many things I love: connecting with others, sharing stories, learning about culture and history, using my communication skills as the conduit between hearts. Encounters like this one inspire me and give me feelings of hope that the world is a wonderful place of a magical human exchange that fuels us to go and grow.

But we had talked so long that it was almost time for lunch, an unrushed 2:00 pm in Spain. When I finally looked at my watch and realized this, the magic spell was broken. They invited me to stay for lunch. Ofelia had made "caldo de verduras" with fresh vegetables that they had grown in their garden. She had also baked fresh bread and "polvorones," Spanish cookies made with walnuts. I politely declined, several times, and finally they acquiesced. But they were not going to let me leave hungry, so they prepared a picnic lunch for me to take along: apples, some of José Manuel's favorite drink, Fanta Naranja, some polvorones and bread. Then, as Ofelia finished gathering these provisions, José Francisco emerged from the back of the shop with a jar in his hands. They were walnuts from the tree in their backyard, and he had spent all morning shelling them.

Cupping the mason jar in his hands, he made a sacred gesture of offering to me, and he told the story of the family walnut tree and how he picked walnuts every day. Then, he shared the best way he had learned to shell them. More magic! But I couldn't possibly accept this gift, as it had so much meaning and took so much time to prepare. I politely refused again, several times. This time, though, José Francisco refused my refusal. He gently placed them in my hands, and then, cupping his around mine, he said, "It is the small things in life that we can share with others that make the biggest difference. You will be hungry, and you will need to eat and drink to make your way on the Camino."

And then, as often is the case in translating from one language to another, there is a feeling behind the words that cannot be translated, especially secondhand and after the fact. The energy behind the words can only be transmitted from one heart to another. José Francisco left me with this: "Qué Diós le bendiga y que las experiencas de su vida alimenten el espíritu como esta comida alimenta el cuerpo. El alimento más profundo: el amor." The best English translation I can offer is this: "May God bless you and may the experiences in your life feed your spirit like this food will nourish your body...the most profound food of all... love."

Wow. Did I ever feel that radiating from them. El amor. I felt like I had bathed in it! As valuable as they would turn out to be, the socks and sandals would be the least of the gifts his family had given me that day.

I hugged all three and thanked them a million times for the food and the shoes and their time. As I finally started out the door, Ofelia followed me, saying that she wanted to walk with me for a while. With another glance at my watch, I told her that I needed to walk fast to try to make up for lost time

"Time is never lost, and it is always well spent," she replied with a wry smile. More wisdom to put in my heart—not my backpack—and carry with me.

Even at almost 80 years old, Ofelia could walk faster than me! We chatted some about her, but mostly she wanted to know more about me and what my life had been like as a teacher and as a mother. With every question she asked, I got the impression she might be living out some dreams of her life through my stories. Maybe she wanted to be a teacher. Maybe she wanted to travel to the U.S., or visit different places and meet all kinds of new people.

After about a half an hour lost in conversation, we had reached the edge of town. I slowed down to say goodbye to Ofelia before she turned back, but instead she veered off the Camino and away from the yellow arrows. *Wait, where was she going?* I followed her, and there it was…the bus station.

She told me that it had gotten so late and that I would never make it to my next stop on the Camino before it got dark, so she wanted me to take a bus. I stood, frozen in my new sandals, which were so comfortable, by the way, that I hardly noticed my blisters or missing toenails.

I didn't know what to feel about the bus station. Deceived that I had been led astray and off my path on the Camino? A sense of failure for wandering so far off my timeline? Shame and inauthenticity for "cheating" *yet again* on this journey? I couldn't be a real pilgrim if I took public transport on a personal journey!

Stubbornly, I hung onto my misconceptions of achievement, and told Ofelia as much.

She just shrugged. "Sometimes our path takes us places we didn't expect, and we just have to figure it out and make the best of it. There's no right or wrong. It just is what it is, and it is meant to be. Our path has been created by God, so just keep going and have faith."

Then, for the third time, there was more negotiating and refusal about buying the ticket. Ofelia, of course, was planning on buying it for me, but eventually I convinced her I would buy it myself, and got on the bus. As we drove away, she watched, waved, and blew me kisses.

I will never forget her, or my time spent with her family. It completely shifted something in me that would also shift my experience of the Camino. I will forever be grateful for that, even if I did have to take a bus. The bus ride was not long, of course— maybe about 30 minutes, which would have taken me five or six hours to walk.

Buoyed by my interactions with Sandra, Victor, Christy, and the Blanco family, I tried chatting with my seat neighbor on the bus. I got as far as finding out her name was Nancy, and she was from Rochester.

"Oh, my aunt lives in Rochester!" I offered with enthusiasm. Yes, a point of connection!

The corners of Nancy's mouth turned down. "Everyone has an aunt that lives in Rochester." Just like that, the connection was denied.

After experiencing all the love from the Blanco family, interacting with Nancy felt like touching a porcupine quill. She was obviously suffering, and I wondered if she was angry that she had to take a bus. Our conversation didn't go any further; she turned her body sideways and closed her eyes, indicating that she didn't want to talk or interact.

I've always felt so rejected when someone did this, internalizing it as a personal slight. But my "lentes nuevos" from the Camino thus far, capped with the experience I'd just had with this loving family, gave me the courage to open my heart and send her love that she might heal those wounds. Physical and emotional, they were causing her to close up, shut down, and isolate herself from the beautiful light that surrounded her, shining from all the luceras along the way.

20

Lessons learned

20.1 Personal Reflection Activity

Not all gifts in life are material ones. We all have gifts to share with the world that are a part of ourselves that help us to be "luceras" to others. Write down as many words that describe the "gifts" that you impart on others each day. (Example: patience, guidance...)

20.2 Interpersonal Connection Activity

Make a list of the top 10 more important things you need in life. Share your list with a partner and discuss, comparing and contrasting with theirs. Fill in the Venn diagram below.

MATTERS OF THE HEART

me   my friend

21

PRAYERS, A PRIEST AND A BROTHER

*"Deep listening is miraculous for both listener and speaker.
When someone receives us with open-hearted, non-judging,
intensely interested listening, our spirits expand."*

—SUE PATTON THOELE, AUTHOR

AFFIRMATION:

*I listen, I pause, I reflect, and then, I repeat the process
until my heart is still and full of love.*

I had now crossed over from the region of Castilla y León
into Galicia, where the Camino finishes. Castilla y León is known
as the region of castles and kings and the center of power, which
even to this day is represented by the castles and lions found on
the official flag of Spain. Geographically, it is a landlocked region
characterized by the meseta and its extreme weather conditions.
Culturally, a great deal of what we learn about Spanish history
occurred in this region. The third oldest university in the world,
the University of Salamanca, was founded here. As a result,
it was considered the center of knowledge and learning, and
is where Columbus went to seek sponsorship to "India" from
Queen Isabella and King Ferdinand. Segovia can also be found in
Castilla y León, with its famous Roman aqueduct and the Alcázar,
the fortress where Isabella was crowned queen and where she
took refuge and stood her ground against the invasion of the

"infidel" African Moors. One could complete their regional tour wandering the grounds of La Granja, the royal summer retreat modeled after the luxurious French palace of Versailles. Castilla y León has always been a region of power and excess. It's no wonder that it tests a pilgrim's willpower and decision-making.

Galicia, on the other hand, is a region defined by its rugged coastline and rainy weather, which distinguish it from the rest of Spain. The temperatures are cooler, and the rain makes for fertile farmland and grazing land for cattle. The terrain of Galicia is almost mystical, not only because of its verdant and hazy aura, but also because it's so different from its neighboring regions. The name Galicia comes from the word "Gallaeci," the ancient Celtic people living in this region. You might remember that they speak a language called "gallego," a mix between Castilian Spanish and Portuguese, and that they believe in Celtic symbols and rituals. They are not known for bullfighting, paella or sangria like the rest of Spain; they are more in tune with the land and the spirit. I have truly crossed over from one cultural spirit to another, and I feel more kinship with the Galician culture.

My first night in Galicia, I rested my feet and reread the Pilgrim's Prayer that Liliana had given me. Then, I went out to attend the pilgrim's mass at the local chapel. After it ended, I lingered in the pews for a few moments, then moved to sit in front of the statue of the Virgin Mary. I looked up into her eyes and suddenly felt shame and guilt.

Where was that coming from? *No, not again!* Then, I noticed the voices chattering in my head. They were those of people who had told me I should have trained more. I should walk faster. I was cheating if I took a cab. I was never going to make it. I shrunk down into the pew and began to cry. Tears blurring my vision, I looked up again at the statue of Mary. This time as I gazed into her eyes, I felt a shift. The voices changed; my energy changed. Now, there was a soothing, singular voice that softly said, "You're okay." "You are enough." "You'll get through this." "Have faith in yourself and who you are. I am always with you."

Okay, where was *that* coming from? Feeling increasingly gobsmacked, I wiped my tear-stained face and once more dared to look up into her eyes. Now they were soothing, loving, and full of compassion. I felt that feeling of unconditional love that a mother has for a child, something that I had never quite experienced, but that I'd always felt a calling to give, both to my own children and the children in my classroom. No conditions, just pure love that frees the spirit to be. Love that guides us to the sweet spot of "I AM" and nothing more. A complete sentence. A subject and a verb, no other nouns or adjectives needed. The power of I AM is all we need, as we are enough. We are complete just existing.

I reflected back to the feelings I had when I first retired. Tired all over again, not jubilant! Because I couldn't put a title on a name tag, I felt I no longer had a purpose that defined who I was or what I did. I searched for more nouns and verbs to add to my "I am" sentence. But it was an endless journey on life's treadmill leading nowhere. I was the proverbial dog chasing its tail, or the ball in the pinball machine bouncing from one flapper to another, or the hamster on the wheel. I had not realized that "I am" was a complete sentence, and whatever I was seeking, I did not need. It was a pursuit of the ego, not the self.

Shortly after I retired, in an attempt to find some direction in the too-quiet aftermath of a fulfilling career, I went to a weekend retreat led by Eckhart Tolle and Kim Eng. Eckhart Tolle talked about presence and said to just "chop the wood and carry the water." Impacted deeply by the retreat, I knew those words were simple and profound, but I didn't clearly appreciate the true meaning of them until now.

On the Camino, I was living that philosophy. Every day was a new day and a new opportunity to take a few more steps toward Santiago. I was grateful for that and the basic joys of life: a good conversation with another pilgrim, a cold stream to comfort my feet, the cool air and a warm sun, a hot "caldo gallego" at the end of my day, talking to my family back home, a body that was still somehow moving me forward on this journey. I was learning to live in the present moment and enjoy all the gifts (or presents!) held within each one.

I returned to my lodging for the night, which was a "casa rural." It was beautifully restored and decorated, and I felt as if I had been transported to another time period. I went down for dinner, which is late in Spain. The dining area was in a small room off the kitchen, certainly not changed or renovated with the latest trends—open floor plan concept, stainless steel appliances, or granite countertops! It was rustic and primitive, but functional, and the food was delicious and all homemade and presented to us like an offering of love.

As I waited for my meal, I felt gratitude about how, on the Camino at the end of the day, I was able to savor the food and take my time to enjoy the dining experience. The innkeeper brought me a steaming hot bowl of stew— not the typical caldo gallego. He cupped the bowl with both hands and served it up to me ceremoniously. I wondered how he was not burning his hands. He smiled, bowed, and said, "Buen provecho."

"Mm, yummy and something different!" I declared out loud, without realizing.

The two men across from me perked up and looked over at me in response. "Ah, you speak English?"

Because I'm a language teacher, I've always been fascinated by the phenomenon that when we hear someone speak our language in another country, we are immediately drawn to them because they're familiar, which we think is comfortable and safe. It turned out that the two men were brothers and they were Canadian, which is nowhere near Florida in the slightest—and yet, here we were, bonding over our shared language. And not just English! I had noticed earlier that they had been speaking French, so I spoke to them in French as well. They were delighted, and I was grateful to have the opportunity to practice my French, and in Spain of all places!

It was truly an authentic exercise in "code switching" between multiple languages in one conversation—a real goosebump, tingler moment for a language teacher. The innkeeper didn't speak much English, so I interpreted in Spanish for the two brothers and answered back in French. I felt like I was living the *I Love Lucy* episode where Lucy has to plead her way out of a Parisian jail with a translation "line" between English and French by way of Spanish and German, thanks to her Cuban husband Ricky and a bilingual drunkard at the police station. It's one of my favorites, and I showed the translation line clip to my students every year, which they laughed at with great enthusiasm and delight!

One of the brothers, Thomas, was retired military, but had spent the last 14 years in administration. He hated the negativity, bullies and bureaucracy, then got sick and retired early. How painfully familiar! It was Thomas's 65th birthday, and he was anxious to finish eating and go into town to celebrate with some pilgrims he had met on the Camino.

By contrast, his brother Anthony was in a lot of pain and not at all interested in going into town or walking any more than he had to. The exchange of their conversation was interesting. Thomas, who was very fit, didn't understand why his brother was in so much pain and "just couldn't push through it." Rather than protest this, Anthony simply agreed with his brother. But he demonstrated pain from his words, and also a great deal of shame that he, indeed, was not enough in his brother's eyes.

Eventually Thomas suggested they could take a cab to the plaza where the party was going to be. "Gee whiz, can't you even walk from the cab to the bar for my birthday? Is that too much to ask or are you that selfish and weak?"

Anthony continued to slump further into his chair, not touching his food. Finally, Thomas looked at his watch and pushed away from the table in anger. "Fine! I'll celebrate my 65th birthday with my new friends!" And he left.

I looked over at Anthony, who had started crying. I was completely unsure of what to do or say, so I just sat there and sent him as much love from my heart that I could muster. He turned to me, wiping his eyes, and said. "I have been a priest all my life. 35 years now. I came on this journey with my brother because I have lost myself and my purpose."

A priest?! Needless to say, this shocked me. I had in no way expected this man to be a priest. The Camino seemed like a place for spirit-seeking journeyers, and to me, priests had all the answers to life's spiritual questions. But here this priest was, speaking the very words that had been running rampant through my head since I had retired three years earlier.

Anthony told me that he and his brother had a difficult relationship and that they had gone in very different directions in their lives. But now they had something in common: they were both lost. He went on to say that he thought this journey would help them both find their way back together. He wiped away the tears streaming down his face, and started his story at the beginning. He told me why he had gone into the priesthood despite the fact that his high school principal refused to write a recommendation for him to apply for seminary. When he asked the principal why, he had told Anthony that he was not very bright and would never make it in college or any other higher education, so don't bother trying because it would just lead to disappointment and disillusion.

Stories like this always get under my skin. To me, it is the ultimate sin of an educator to tell a child that they are not smart, not good enough, or not capable of achieving anything they want to do. We dress them down with disempowering words of shame and guilt, and then don't understand why they can't seem to measure up to our standards. Over the years, I've seen many times that the parents, teachers, friends, or relatives that do this often don't feel enough themselves. It's not about the other person in the slightest.

So often we adults expect young people to know what they want and somehow find it without the necessary support and guidance as to how to make the best choices that fit their needs. But the truth of the matter is that many young people need adults to advocate for them, to show them the way forward, to impart hard-fought wisdom—exactly as José Francisco had said.

Well, Anthony had felt the same way, so he told that principal that his job was to do everything in his power to help Anthony as a student. He didn't have to lie, but he DID have to write a recommendation that would at the very least TRY to make a difference in the life of a student. He also reminded the principal that every child has a gift and a passion, and that his was to help others who were in need.

Anthony was looking for hope. That is all any of us is looking for, and it is up to each and every one of us to give that to a child who is just beginning their journey. Every choice, every intention, every step we take makes a difference. Anthony knew that, and that's the gift he wanted to share with the world to make it a better place. He had faith...faith in humanity...in his and in that of others. He felt he could best do that through his role as a priest, so that was the path he chose. He continued to explain how he had been so enthusiastic and passionate about being a priest and helping people find their way through their pains, sorrows and "sins." He had felt very rewarded by the healing power of connection with his congregation, like he had made a difference in the world, and was truly serving God and His purpose.

However, as time went on, there were more and more restrictions and interventions from the church that prevented him from truly connecting with the people. He was doing more connecting with paperwork, meetings, the computer, and the red tape of bureaucracy than with the hearts of the people. He felt isolated and disempowered from his true self and his true purpose. The church seemed unwilling to change this situation, which made Anthony feel even more cut off and held back from his healing work. After 35 years, he was considering leaving the priesthood and breaking his vow to God—his purpose. A parallel track to so many disenchanted and burned out teachers considering leaving the profession.

Anthony continued talking, releasing all that was in his heart and soul, feelings of failure and betrayal and sacrilege. I listened and offered gentle words of understanding and affirmation. It was a real role reversal, yet it felt familiar. It felt like all the times I listened to colleagues and students who were struggling through their days, and just listened and nodded as they unburdened their hearts. Anthony finally declared that he was going to go home in the morning despite his brother's protests. He felt at peace with himself and with God and wanted to go home.

He didn't say what he was going to do after that. I had a feeling he was going to leave the priesthood and do some one-on-one counseling, but I never found out. My hope for him is the same as my hope for everyone struggling against the binding ties of institutional red tape: to restore his heart to its true purpose, which is sharing love, peace, compassion, and forgiveness.

21

Lessons learned

21.1 Personal Reflection Activity

Write a letter to your younger self and "confess" all the things that you wish you had done differently and why. Then, explain in what ways the things you did turned out, in hindsight, to be the "best" decision or outcome possible that has led to where you are today.

21.2 Interpersonal Connection Activity

We all have favorite childhood storybooks. Retell the story in your own words to a partner. The role of the partner is to then only listen for the details of "who," "what," "where," "when," "why," and "how," and complete a chart of these details. The partner may use facial expressions, gestures and other body cues to prompt communication, but they may not speak. Look at the details written down by the partner and discuss anything that is different or inaccurate or missing. How are your interpretations of the story different? The same? Why do you think that is?

WHO?	WHAT?	WHERE?	WHEN?	WHY?	HOW?

22

ANTAGONISTS AND RIVALS
(HELLO, EGO!)

"The ego is a screen made of mental conditioning or past identification with thoughts and emotions through which we see and act on the world."

—ECKHART TOLLE, SPIRITUAL TEACHER

AFFIRMATION:

I go deep within myself to find truth and peace beyond the chatter of all those conditioned and repetitive thoughts in my head.

Walking further into Galicia, my blisters had mostly healed, and I was keeping a pretty steady pace. The days were cool and the nights cold—at least to me, a gal from Florida. Mist rolled in over the gentle sloping hills and the temperature dropped to the 40s at night. In the morning, the sun came up around 8:00 am, yet I didn't want to get out from under the warm and weighted swaddle of the covers. I could see my breath even *inside* my room! All of my accommodations were devoid of TVs or internet (and sometimes even climate control devices like heat or air conditioning!), which gave me an opportunity to reflect on how much technology has become so integrated into our lives that we believe it to actually be a necessity.

Helped by the absence of digital distractions, I continued to write in my journal and reflect on my day. There was a stillness and deep peace that permeated me during the evenings spent reflecting and writing. It even carried over during the day, too, as I walked alone in contemplation, appreciating the beauty of Galicia around me. Instead of counting sheep, I counted cows. Finally, I was no longer afraid to be alone or left behind, so my monkey mind had left the circus for now...at least until I invited another circus to town. But I was trying very hard not to do that. I wanted to be a lucera, living more in gratitude, peace, joy and compassion, for myself and for others that I met along the way.

As is often the case of lessons newly learned, I had perhaps lulled myself into a false sense of accomplishment. The next people I would meet along the Camino would shake me to the core. Yet again, they were two Canadian sisters—not Edith and Dolores that I had met my first day out on the Camino, but Joan and Susan. These two sisters were younger, and from Ottawa. They had noticed that we had been at the same posadas for a few nights now, and asked if they could join me for lunch.

Sister Maya Angelou once said, "When people show you who they are, believe them the first time." I wish I'd been mindful of that during my first lunch with Joan and Susan, because it wasn't long into our conversation of niceties before we were all showing who we truly were. The interaction would pivot away from the opportunity to act with consideration of Sister Maya's wisdom, and towards the painful opportunity to reflect on the lesson that I was getting back what I projected into the world. Joan and Susan immediately tapped into the feelings of "not good enough" that I had been struggling with during the whole Camino. What I still needed to learn was that my Ego is what kept showing up to rescue me from my fear, and until I was willing and able to consciously let it go, I would suffer. Opportunity #9,999 in my life to try to learn this lesson. What kind of feedback would I get on my report card for this lifelong class I kept failing? Was I constantly seeking affirmation that I was "special," or a victim?

Just as I had lulled myself into a false sense of self-esteem, these two women took me down, *hard*. After the niceties were over, their questions seemed to grow deliberate, directly tapping into my shadow side that I thought had been enlightened by my experiences so far on the Camino. Like my first Spanish class in junior high school, I had learned all my lessons, gotten an "A," and didn't need to retake the class, right? But entering into the equation were new variables, and more challenging practice to work through the problem.

I told them how I had suffered so much with blisters, and they told me how they didn't have any. I told them that I had changed from boots to sandals, and they said that sandals with socks looked ridiculous. "Don't you know that you have to let your feet breathe and take off the socks? Or better yet, wear tennis shoes that allow your feet to naturally breathe. That's what we're doing."

I told them how I had trained in the hot sun of Florida, but that didn't prepare me for the challenges of the mountains. They said they didn't even train before they came. "How could you think the terrain of Spain would be like that of Florida? That's just ridiculous!"

They told me they knew they couldn't carry so much weight in a backpack and how could any fool be so naive as to think that they could do that. They told me they had a friend who was supposed to accompany them, but she was not physically fit enough (she was older and overweight like me), but she didn't come because she knew she would hold the sisters back. I pointed out that she could have taken a cab when she couldn't walk anymore, like I had.

They both gasped in shock. "You can't take a cab on the Camino! That's cheating!"

Shame.

A sick feeling rose in my gut and all the energy drained from my body. I immediately stood up, holding back the tears, and left the table. Back in my room, I cried my eyes and heart out for hours. The monkey mind was back, and this time it brought the whole three-ring circus of self-loathing and shame.

The next day, the sisters waited for me after breakfast so that the three of us could walk together. *When people show you who they are, believe them the first time.* I kept pace with them for a bit, but it wasn't long before they made it clear that I was holding them back. So they walked ahead, leaving me in the dust. I would see them eventually up the road at a bar, resting and having drinks. Then, in the evening, I would see them again, and foolishly agree to have dinner with them. (I know, I know. *When people show you who they are, believe them the first time.*)

By now, each stage of the Camino was about 23-25 kilometers (14-15 miles), and I began to see Susan and Joan starting to show signs of tiredness and sore muscles, but of course they would never admit to it. Susan was especially struggling with calf problems going downhill. They also struggled with the language. Joan especially was not comfortable trying to communicate with waiters or shop owners. It was here where I regained some of my self-worth in their presence. I had the invaluable ability to speak Spanish. So Joan would dictate, "Tell them that I want blah-blah-blah," and I would relay the message. At one point, she even groused, "My gosh! I don't know why they don't speak English. Everyone speaks English these days. It's the international language."

When people show you who they are, believe them the first time. I had spent an entire career combatting that philosophy. I had sought to show my students how knowing another language beyond English was a way to enrich their lives through connection.

Joan complained about everything they had or didn't have in Spain and how "backward" they were. "It's really a third world country," she said. I winced at every complaint she leveled. Then, there was the money. Every time she and Susan paid, they were so inconvenienced that they had to figure out how much money they had, and how to convert it to the Canadian dollar. "And what's up with this Monopoly money, anyway?!"

When people show you who they are, believe them the first time. So why was I spending so much of my time with Joan and Susan, who embodied values so different from my own? Maybe I wasn't practiced enough at speaking up and going off on my own. Maybe I was still afraid. Maybe, even though they made me feel terrible, they were familiar to me. Maybe I had another lesson to learn.

Throughout all my interactions with her, Joan did not want to show vulnerability in any way. She was closed off to having a real life experience in Spain, and seemed only to be there to check the Camino off her Bucket List. No cultural exchange, no self-reflection, no inward journey. She wanted to stay in complete control of everything and everyone.

Truthfully, she reminded me of my mother, and some of the people in my life with whom I'd had difficulty managing relationships. Usually these people had experienced such hurt and trauma in their childhoods that they lived their lives in self-protection, attacking first before they could be attacked. They would build a fortress the likes of Fort Knox to keep the treasure of who they really were safely buried and locked behind all the walls. No one was getting in there.

I understand the feeling of not wanting to be vulnerable. We all retreat into our "vault" when we are hurt or afraid. What we need to learn to do is not lock the door and throw away the key. When dealing with aggressive people like Joan, I had found that I would lock the door and hide. Run away. I would not set boundaries or speak up to protect myself. But I wasn't quite like the full-time vault-dwellers. I struggled with figuring out to whom I could give a key to that door. Who could I trust to not hurt me?

Compared to Joan, Susan was more open and curious about what she was experiencing in Spain. She had a gentler spirit and showed kindness in her words and interactions with people. It was easy to talk to her and let her in. She asked some questions about Spain, but also made observations and followed up by asking for my take on what she had noticed. Joan was different. Joan wanted to challenge me and the knowledge that made me "smarter" than her in Spain. She would ask questions to see if I had an answer. If I didn't, she would make a flippant gesture or shaming statement, like, "Oh, you don't know that? Seems like something a Spanish teacher should know."

If I *did* know the answer, she then questioned more, or argued with me. If she couldn't come up with a strong follow-up, she would say things like, "Well, aren't you smart?" or "Gee, those students of yours sure were lucky to have such a smart teacher. I bet they really felt dumb, like they would never be able to be as smart."

All of this interaction with Joan and Susan challenged me with a huge and very painful opportunity to reflect on some of the most difficult relationships I'd ever had with family members and colleagues. I realized that a movie reel of my life was playing out on the Camino. I was meeting people along the way that were reflections of the people I'd had relationships and interactions with in my daily life. I was meeting my Self, the shadow side of me in my Ego, the lighter side of me in the Divine. The Camino was the journey of my life, both literally and metaphorically.

What I *still was not getting* was that I could choose whom to walk with and whom to walk away from. The shadow side of me was still afraid. Afraid of disapproval, afraid of not being enough, afraid of confrontation, afraid of abandonment, afraid of not pleasing others, afraid of not being loved. The light side of me was showing up in the inspiration, joy, and hope of people like Liliana, Jaime, the farmer, Santiago, Sandra, Victor, Anthony, and the Blanco family. I was so blessed and grateful to have met them and learned from their loving kindness. But then there were the Joans. Ultimately, I was meeting different parts of myself on the Camino—the dark, the light, all of it.

22

Lessons learned

22.1 Personal Reflection Activity

Who is your favorite superhero and why? What are their strengths? What are their weaknesses? How are you like them or not like them? Is there anyone like them that you know? Who? What role do they play in your life, and yours in theirs?

22.2 Interpersonal Connection Activity

Write a description of a movie pitch to a Hollywood producer in which you convince them to create their next movie based on the superhero duo of you and this role model that you admire. Include the "who," "what," "when," "where," "why," and "how" in your pitch.

23

THE BEAUTY OF GETTING LOST

"Some beautiful paths cannot be discovered without getting lost."

—EROL OZAN, AUTHOR

AFFIRMATION:

I always can find my way when I just pay attention to the signs in front of me and trust the path ahead.

Before I knew it, I reached Sarria, where the majority of pilgrims begin the Camino. Many of the pilgrims starting in Sarria choose to do so out of a matter of convenience. Some of them can't get enough time off work; some have health issues that limit them walking the whole thing. Some, like Joan, are walking the Camino to be able to check it off their Bucket List, and starting in Sarria is the minimum requirement to get your official certificate of completion, the compostela. The compostela was a valuable document to the pilgrims as it was evidence of their penance that they could show not only their family and friends, but also to St. Peter at the gates of Heaven.

Thinking of it this way was less appealing to me. Life can't be reduced to a checklist of boxes to "stamp" with a check. Just because we've arrived at our goal or checked a box does NOT mean we are done learning. Everyone is so busy checking off boxes and getting to the next challenge that we don't really slow down enough to reflect and play along the way. We value accomplishment and we devalue exploration, curiosity, and enjoyment. We don't marvel in the miracles and the gifts of life!

Thankfully, once I had arrived in Sarria, I had a chance to reconnect with Jaime and Liliana. They were staying a couple of days here to meet up with their daughter and a friend, who could only get a week off from work, and walk the rest of the way to Santiago as a group. I met them for dinner, and as always, Liliana was kind and encouraging.

"You are in the home stretch. You have come so far, and you can do it!" Liliana was my ultimate cheerleader on the Camino, and to this day I am endlessly grateful to have met her. We all need those kind of people in our lives! During the meal, she presented everyone with bracelets adorned with the yellow arrow of the Camino, to remind us of our path and the way back to ourselves.

Now that we were less than a week outside of Santiago, the excitement on the Camino was growing palpable. By now I had developed a steady walking rhythm, thanks to my comfy socks and sandals, as well as some mantras to help me be mindful and stay on path. They all were to the tune of other songs, but with words that I made up. In the classroom, they're called "piggyback songs," and I used to use them to help students remember grammar concepts more easily and enjoyably. Here's what I was singing in my head on the Camino.

To the tune of *Frère Jacques*:

I am walking, I am growing

On my path, on my path

To Santiago, to my truth

C'mon let's go, c'mon let's grow.

To the tune of *Mary Had a Little Lamb*:

I am grateful to be here, to be here, to be here

I am grateful to be here

And learning every day.

I also had mantras that were more like prayers, intended to guide me, ask for support, and allay my fears. The most common one (and the one with which I continue to start my day, every day) is to a tune I made up, so it is technically not a piggyback song. The words are:

Dear Heavenly Father, please guide me today

Dear Heavenly Father, and show me the way

Dear Heavenly Father, please help me to see

Dear Heavenly Father, just to be me

And set me free, set me free, set me free.

Music, like art, is a powerful medium for transmitting what can be found deep in the souls of our being, in those treasure chests of emotions that we have hidden away inside of us. Every time I see arts and languages programs sidelined in favor of STEM (science, technology, engineering, and math), I feel a pang of sadness. Of course, STEM subjects are valuable and necessary to learn. But the value we have placed on them to grow our economy is disproportionate to the value that we place on the arts and languages, which are important to grow our humanity.

The "battle" to put the A in STEM and encourage STEAM is ongoing. The ESSA (Every Student Succeeds Act, which followed Race to the Top and No Child Left Behind in federal education laws) promotes balance between STEM and the arts for a more "well-rounded education" (and child). But there are still threats of eliminating ESSA and promoting legislation that supports more computer coding. To boot, some state governments are considering passing laws that would allow these coding classes to be substituted for language requirements. In 2016, I found myself presenting to the Florida state legislature in an effort to convince them that computer language and human language aren't interchangeable. It is still an ongoing discussion.

Technology has the power to connect us, but it can also isolate us. Students nowadays endeavor so much of the learning experience through a screen or a device, and many education initiatives are losing sight of the power of presence. Even despite technology's awesome power to connect, human connection facilitates learning and growth beyond measurable data. But we are so focused on what is good for growing business and the economy. Making more money, gaining more "things." Measuring what does that, doing more of it, and developing the technology to make it more cost effective and efficient.

Throughout my Camino journey, I was disconnected from the artificial world of technology and the constant demand of energy that it brings. Instead I had the privilege of living from my heart and making connections to other humans, from many different languages and cultures, and to the beauty of nature's art and music that surrounded me. Some might say that we cannot sustain this kind of life because we have to work and live in cities or communities that don't allow for this kind of experience. I disagree. Through meditation, mindfulness, and prayer, we can make choices that best serve us and our personal path on the human journey of life. We must find ways to reconnect and stay connected to ourselves, and to others whose relationships benefit us. We must tune in to what is really going on within us so that we can create a circle of life that is sustained by what really matters: love, joy, empathy, compassion and kindness—the music and lyrics of the heart.

My prayer to "Dear Heavenly Father" would soon bring that lesson to life in a huge and meaningful way that would change me forever. It would be the "shift" that would light the way to my True Self. We are all waiting for that shift, in ourselves and others, but for most, it doesn't happen until we see a light shining and take a path that makes it happen.

•   •   •

The next day, I walked in peace, singing my mantras and saying my prayer to Dear Heavenly Father. It was a long day of struggle, and I focused on the songs and words in my mind, putting one foot in front of the other. But after a while, I realized I was no longer seeing the yellow arrows, nor was I coming across other pilgrims on the path.

Oh no.

I was lost.

I have been walking almost three weeks now and I know what to look for, how could I have missed the signs? I checked my guidebook, but it didn't help. I tried my Camino app and even tried to call the hotel to get help, but there was no signal. I was left with only one option: the old-fashioned way. I had to try to find a yellow arrow just by walking around. But even if I stumbled back on path quickly, it was going to be dark soon.

I made my best guess, and walked ten minutes in that direction. No pilgrims, no arrow. I gulped and turned around, plodding back to where I'd begun. I tried another direction... still no arrow. More backtracking.

Now there were no songs in my mind—only prayers, rising in concert with shame and blame and panic. My worst fears had been realized: I was lost. I was alone. I couldn't find my way back.

With the sun lowering ever closer to the horizon, I tried to calm my nerves and trust my gut. With a deep, shaky breath, I set off in a third direction, scanning far and wide for a yellow arrow of signs of another pilgrim.

Finally, I spotted one. The trail emerged with it, and before long I was back on path, following arrow after comforting arrow. Even so, it was hard to shake the feeling of panic and dread that had flooded me.

When I arrived at my hotel, I was greeted by the familiar routine: Joan and Susan had already arrived and were waiting to have dinner with me. Apparently there was a restaurant nearby they had heard was good.

What I really wanted was to hide in my room, collect my thoughts and re-compose myself.

What I really wanted was to say no.

But instead, I said, "Yes." (I know! I KNOW!!!)

Here's what I told myself: I was hungry. I couldn't go to bed without eating, or else I wouldn't sleep well. Sleep is important, food is important.

This is, of course, all true, but another truth was the fact that in no way did I need to eat with Joan and Susan. But I went anyway. And, in the end, I took the energy of my frustration and fear and fallibility to the table, and served it up like a three course meal. In the face of my vulnerability, I was armored up and the hatches were battened down for a stormy ride ahead.

As we sat down, the napkins were no sooner folded in our laps that Joan and Susan asked about my day. "What happened to you? We've been here for hours. What do you mean, you got lost? How could you have gotten lost? The yellow arrows were right there. Didn't you see them?"

Uh-oh. That was all it took. A torrent of emotions and surge of tears came crashing down around me. I lost it, right there, at the dinner table, in the restaurant. Our poor waiter, a young man who surely would have preferred a completely uneventful dinner shift, valiantly attempted to console me as I dissolved into sobs. Joan and Susan, to their credit, were also trying to comfort me, with softer voices and kinder words than they usually used.

"You are doing a great job. You've got this. We almost got lost too! It was a hard day for us too. We are struggling too. You're way too hard on yourself. You've done amazing things, and you're doing this too! You know Spanish and so much about the culture and people here. We wish we knew half as much as you do. You can't quit. You are almost there. You can do it!"

But I couldn't hear them. I was suddenly in the eye of the hurricane of my emotions. The accumulated winds of torment, shame, fear, anger, frustration, and fallibility had gathered enough strength and forward motion to overtake me. These energies had finally built up enough force to stir the pot of "yuck" that had been stewing inside of me for years—not just the journey of the Camino, but the journey that had led me here.

Without a bite to eat, I managed to gather the pieces of me off the floor of the restaurant and slump shamefully to my room, feet aching with every step. When I arrived, I stripped off my sturdy socks and sweat-dried clothes, and took a bath, trying to wash the day off of me. Still crying. Then, the bathwater drained away, I refilled the tub and poured in salt, so I could soak my feet. The stinging pain felt like the proportional reward for my mistakes. Crying and crying.

Finally clean, I lowered myself gingerly onto the edge of the bed, and stared blankly out at the meager view from the balcony. My tears were finally subsiding, and the storm of negative emotions receding. But the damage had been done. There was debris that I had to reckon with, the stirred-up stuff that reared its ugly head and overtook me.

Since the beginning of my Camino journey, I had felt so

much fear of getting lost. I carried it with me in every step of the process: in my oversized backpack, in the company I clung to even if they made me feel bad, in the careful steps and insistence on doing everything right.

I had gotten lost anyway.

And here I was, safely in my hotel room, with a tear-stained face and bandaged socks-and-sandaled feet, only days from my destination. I had been confronted by those fears, and I survived.

But...how much of my journey on the Camino was driven by that fear? How much had that darkness shadowed my experience?

I began to think about why I was even walking across Spain in the first place. What I had been seeking. What I had been missing. How I had gotten off my path after leaving the classroom for the district job. How I had felt utterly lost in "retirement."

How much of *my life* had I lived in fear of being lost, alone, helpless, and abandoned?

It was an illuminating and uncomfortable question to ask.

Whether student or teacher, in school or in my job, I had driven myself to overachievement and exhaustion so that I would not be lost, clueless, or behind. I'd always defer to others, so that I wouldn't feel left out of life's interpersonal connections. I'd feel resentment when no one bothered to reciprocate. I would set no boundaries with anyone so that I could enjoy a false sense of unconditional acceptance. If that didn't work, I negotiated conditions with myself: If I were: a. smarter, b. faster, c. more capable, d. better, e. all of the above, then, *they would* or *I would*... There was always something better to reach if only I changed myself.

As a language teacher, I spent so much time teaching about the subjunctive mood in Spanish—when there's doubt or uncertainty about an outcome. I had put such an emphasis on the *imperfect* subjunctive, which constructs "if... then" sentences, completely mirroring my real-life conditional negotiating. *If I were smarter, faster, more capable, and better,* then the result I wanted *would happen.*

In reality, all of that doubt and uncertainty are made up. So much imperfection and too many conditions of "coulda, shoulda, woulda." It's all hypothetical. It's all a projection of our emotions. It's not real. Not real-ly important, not real-ly true, not real-ly who I am. I had been searching for that imperfect person my whole life, and the reason I was lost was because that person didn't real-ly exist. And the reason she didn't exist was because she was living in the alternate universe of the shadow side of my mind. I was chasing a ghost, trying to escape from a haunted house I had constructed around me. I was lost in the labyrinth of my not-enoughness. How would I ever find my way out? How would I get there? What if, what if, what if? Fear, fear, fear.

I thought back through my life, looking for the places where my fear of being lost or alone manifested. I ended up at the source. My mother had had a tough job taking care of four children, two of which were in diapers and one who was in a wheelchair. I was the one in the middle, needing the least attention and care, so I never really got that from her. Her attention was too consumed with her other children, and she didn't have any extra to give to me.

Unconditional parental love—without the qualifications of "if...then"—is all that any of us crave throughout our whole childhood. And if we don't get it, we will spend the rest of our adult lives trying to find it and "earn" it. That is where our feelings of "not-enoughness" stem from. Getting lost and not having someone there to help me or rescue me or protect me was the deepest fear I had on the Camino. Every day, I walked my way through the unknown, the unpredictable, the uncontrollable and the unexpected. What else to do but fear?

Moreover, my fear was causing me to play the victim. I had once read about the Karpman Drama Triangle, a social model of human interaction that maps a type of destructive interaction that can occur between people in conflict. It identifies victim, rescuer and persecutor at each point of the triangle. I wondered now if the triangle also applies to our relationship with ourselves. The voice in our head bounces from one tip of the triangle to another, speaking from each role, depending on what is going on outside of our selves, our Ego. It generates the appropriate scripted dialogue for the role we're playing today: the victim, the rescuer, or the persecutor.

In the stillness and quiet of my room, the storm had finally cleared and my breathing returned to normal. A kind of calm had washed over me, a new kind of peacefulness. I surrendered to everything that had been exposed in the restaurant that night. I had gotten lost, and I found my way back. I had figured it out and made it to safety. Every step, every mis-step and every perceived "fall-failure" on the Camino and in my life had served as a lesson on the way to my destination. With each step, each person and each experience, I had been given the opportunity to self-reflect and learn a personalized, meaningful lesson.

When I began the Camino, I was in the realm of "what if?" I had been seeking something I thought I lacked. But I've never lacked anything. I had lived my life thinking I needed to do more, be more, be different in order to be enough.

But I knew now that wasn't true. I had been blessed with amazing grace. I had moved past the false sense of uncertainty and entered the present tense. I was able to do what I'd always struggled with: let go and let flow. I was a lucera, lighting the way not just for others, but for myself.

23

Lessons learned

23.1 Personal Reflection Activity

Think of an experience or situation in which you played the role of one of the points on the Karpman Drama Triangle. Explain what was happening and how you were fulfilling that role. Then, fill in the other two points with the names of the other people involved in the drama and how they were fulfilling their roles. What could maybe have been done differently in order to abate any drama happening?

RESCUER

VICTIM

PERSECUTOR

23.2 Interpersonal Connection Activity

Create a work of art...that can serve as an inspiration to help someone you know who is struggling right now. Gift them your ART from the heART.

my gift of heART

24

AMAZING GRACE

"Amazing Grace, How sweet the sound
That saved a wretch like me
I once was lost, but now am found
T'was blind but now I see
T'was Grace that taught my heart to fear
And Grace, my fears relieved
How precious did that grace appear
The hour I first believed
Through many dangers, toils and snares
We have already come.
T'was grace that brought us safe thus far
And grace will lead us home,
And grace will lead us home
Amazing grace, How sweet the sound
That saved a wretch like me
I once was lost but now am found
T'was blind but now I see
Was blind, but now I see."

—CELTIC HYMN

AFFIRMATION:

I live in grace and gratitude and
experience all that is amazing in life.

Energized by my epiphany, I left the next morning with the song *Amazing Grace* already in my head. Alone, and not the least bit afraid. I didn't expect Joan and Susan to be anywhere in sight after last night. It was uncomfortable for everyone near our table. But that was okay. I wasn't thinking of anything or anyone. I was just walking, taking in my surroundings, and enjoying the experience of that moment. I wasn't dwelling on what happened earlier on the Camino, or worrying about what was coming up on the Camino. I was just on the Camino, in Spain, having a once-in-a-lifetime experience that, after this moment, would be gone, and after the next, would be gone, and so on.

The lyrics of the song turned over in my head, and reflected back to me in my surroundings. In this present moment, everything was amazing! Amazing, amazing, amazing. I was meeting amazing people along the way. I was having an amazing experience. And the beauty of life that surrounded me in Nature was amazing.

"Amazing," derived from the verb "amaze," means "causing great surprise or wonder. I like to think of it as the feeling of wholeness and enlightenment that we experience after going through "a maze" of problems, obstacles, and falls. I could see my maze clearly now, as though I finally had a bird's-eye view that revealed every dead end, trick path, and double-back. I had been stuck in the twists and turns of a false self that would never, ever be enough. It raced from one illusion to another, trying to figure out which way would magically change everything and answer all my problems. I'd only end up exhausted and more lost.

In teacher terms, I had been approaching life like an assessment or test. It was either multiple choice, true/false, or fill-in-the-blanks. I would freeze in fear that I wouldn't choose that ONE RIGHT POWERFUL ANSWER on a multiple choice test. I worried that I would choose true when it was false or vice versa, then regret my decision and beat myself up for not knowing.

Then, there was the fill-in-the-blank portion of my life: every time I felt I didn't do well on an assessment—usually determined by my own rubric, comparing myself to others—the voice in my head would generate a long list of negative and disempowering adjectives to finish the sentence "I am _____." The two most powerful and creative words that exist: "I am..."

I am stupid.

I am incompetent.

I am slow. I am behind. I am ugly. I am fat. And so on.

Then, I would find evidence to support these proclamations and reaffirm the negative adjectives. "I can't." "I won't." "I could've, I should've, I would've." This is the essay portion of the assessment, where I try to make sense of everything. What is my "main idea" of who I am or I'm not? Now let's examine my past and future to seek out evidence-based examples, and give supporting details to prove the main idea.

No wonder we reach negative conclusions about ourselves when we're using this assessment. And no wonder we get stuck in mazes of our own design, seeking a definitive solution to our lost-ness, an exit where perhaps there isn't one. Perhaps this is the wisdom behind Joseph Campbell's most famous quote, which had long fascinated me with its enigmatic advice: "Follow your bliss, and the Universe will open doors where there were only walls."

We can't find true happiness and live in a state of bliss when we are always striving for concrete answers to all our perceived problems. The REAL and only TRUE answer to finding bliss is to live in the powerful present moment of I AM. To be curious and open to follow the wonder and wander in your heart, not your mind. To lose our illusions of life as merely a test and embrace the reality of life as a personal adventure to be explored with wonder. It's the ultimate path to truth and to living in the bliss of who we really are and why we are really here. When we live in a state of bliss, life just flows, and we float along with it.

As I was floating along on the Camino that morning, I came upon a young girl walking very slowly and limping. Coming up beside her, I decided to say hello.

"Do you speak Spanish?" I asked, in Spanish.

She said "no," and answered in Italian.

But that wouldn't necessarily rule out conversation. Spanish and Italian are so similar, I'd been able to use Spanish without difficulty on a trip to Rome with my husband just a few months before. So I asked some questions in Spanish, and she answered reluctantly in Italian. I found out that her name was Thomasina, 19 years old and from Rome. Thrilled about the chance to chat about the city, I continued asking questions and talking about how much I loved my recent trip there.

But the conversation dropped off before long, and Thomasina's gaze was glued to her feet the whole time. Grasping for another connection, I asked if she spoke any English. At this question, she actually stopped, turning to look at me with surprise and trepidation. Then she shook her head slowly.

"School."

I think she thought this downbeat answer would deter me. But, much to her surprise, I took that and ran with it! In language learning, when you're communicating with someone who isn't proficient in the language, there's a key skill called "sympathetic listening" that can enhance their success—and more importantly, their confidence. A sympathetic listener increases the likelihood that the speaker will be understood by reiterating, rephrasing and reformulating the information they're receiving. In my experience, these are the REAL three "R"s of learning that should happen in school! Additionally, a sympathetic listener uses gestures, context clues, and inference to make connections and achieve better understanding of the message. Communication is slow and deliberate, and there are frequent pauses for reflection, clarification, and negotiation of meaning.

So, ready to step into this role, I reiterated her answer. "Oh, you took English in school?"

She nodded. "Yes." A pause, then: "No good."

Normally my next question is a more emotions-based, personalized one: "Did you like it?" But I didn't even need to ask it because it was obvious from Thomasina's demeanor that she'd had a terrible experience learning English in school.

So I asked a different question instead. "Do you want to learn English?"

"Of course, I like American movies and TV."

Ah, there was my way in! "Well, today is your lucky day! I'm a language teacher, and I can practice English with you, if you'd like. You can say whatever you want, and I will understand you. Okay?"

After a moment, Thomasina agreed. Though she didn't feel confident in her language skills, I felt confident in my ability to encourage her. She was so familiar to me, from my experience as a teacher as well as my experience as a student. The two things that hold a student back, particularly in learning another language, are 1) the fear of making a mistake, and 2) fear of looking or feeling stupid. Both of these fears lead back to the unwillingness to be vulnerable in their lack of proficiency, and a falsely assumed label of "not good enough."

Because I experienced these fears as a student myself, I was intuitively sensitive to this as a teacher. It made me inherently suited for sympathetic listening, because my main goal in communication was to help learners feel at ease to take a risk and let go of their fears. I wanted learners to feel loved and validated, perhaps nurturing my own inner child who hadn't felt that support as a young person.

To help put Thomasina at ease, I started by asking all the questions, and using my sympathetic listener super powers to keep the conversation and the connection going. But as we walked more, she began to say more and more in English. I quickly discovered that she knew a lot more than she was willing to let on. She was so afraid of making a mistake and being misunderstood. If she had overstated her skills, it would open the door to judgment and failure, so she downplayed her real abilities.

After several hours at a gentle pace, Thomasina was telling me about her favorite TV shows (*Gilmore Girls*) and her favorite superhero character (*Wonder Woman*). She even shared more personal details about her life, like how she had moved out of her parents' house, even though it wasn't culturally common. In Europe, children stayed with their parents until well into their 30s. At 18, Thomasina wanted to go to university, but she hadn't done well enough in school to be able to fulfill that wish. So, she moved out, got a job, and was living in a tiny one-room apartment in Rome.

"What is your job?" I asked.

Her head ducked again, and her voice got quiet. "Cleaning."

I assumed this meant she was a maid or housekeeper working in the hospitality industry, like Victor and Sandra. "Oh, which hotel?"

Her reply was even quieter. "Streets...I clean garbage in streets."

"Oh," I said, feeling foolish for the incorrect assumption.

"No good job. I'm stupid."

Well, I would have none of that! In my classroom, no student was no good. No student was ever stupid. I leapt into teacher-counselor mode. "No one is stupid. Everyone has a job to do in life, and every job is important to society and the good of others. My husband and I were just in Rome, and we were amazed at how clean the streets were, unlike other big cities. If there's a lot of trash in the streets and on the metro, it leaves us with a bad impression of those cities. As a street cleaner, you are a goodwill ambassador to tourism and a source of pride for your city to keep it so clean and leave everyone with such good impressions of Rome. You have an important job."

We had slowed to a stop, so I could look Thomasina directly in the eye. "Really?" she said, still in disbelief.

"*Really!*" I began to tell her about several of my former students who had not gone to college, but who were doing things that made them happy and that were contributing to the greater good of the people around them, and society as a whole.

We began walking along again, and I searched for another topic of conversation. "I like your tattoo," I ventured. An image of the Cheshire Cat from *Alice in Wonderland* covered the entire calf on Thomasina's left leg. It was surrounded by the quote: "How long is forever? Sometimes just one second."

I was curious about the choice of quote, because if I remembered *Alice in Wonderland* correctly, it was said by the White Rabbit, not the Cheshire Cat. From a teacher standpoint, I wasn't sure if Thomasina could articulate the meaning of her tattoo, given her limited English, but my personal curiosity won out.

"Isn't that from *Alice in Wonderland*?"

"Yes," she said.

"Is that your favorite Disney movie?"

"Yes."

Then, I went for the deeper question: "Why?"

More than *what, who, when, where,* or *how, why* is always the most difficult question to answer in any conversation, whether it is with another person or with ourselves. It requires the deepest thought and articulation of meaning from the perspective of intention. We must examine our intentions to communicate them, and when this awareness of our intentions leads to making choices that align with them.

"Why?" is the most meaningful question we can ask in the learning journey. In the classroom, we might ask "why?" but usually we simply seek a scripted answer copied from the book. The answer we think is "right." We do not give children enough time, space, meaningful experiences or permission for exploring and discovering answers for themselves and figuring out their own answers to "why?" We are teaching to the test, and they are memorizing and being programmed for the test. Asking "why?" allows for exploration that is personalized and meaningful, and promotes reflection and connection to what is inside and outside of our being. As long as we have the freedom to ask "why?" and know that there is no "perfectly right" answer, we will be curious and explore and learn.

Even though Thomasina's vocabulary and language skills were limited in English, her thoughts were not, and her passion about her tattoo wasn't either. She communicated through few words that the Rabbit was always in a hurry and trying to please everyone. She sometimes felt like that. On the other hand, the Cheshire Cat was both funny and scary at the same time, and that life was like that for her sometimes. She used that quote to remind her that none of it was real or forever because everything in life can change in a second. Nothing is permanent, nothing is real, nothing is forever, so "go with the flow."

"Seguire la corrente," she summarized in Italian. She smiled a big smile that was reminiscent of the Cheshire Cat.

•　　•　　•

The next day I continued walking with Thomasina. It was a particularly frustrating day because there were bicycles riding on the foot path of the Camino. By the time we finally found a place to stop for lunch, it was nearly 4:00 pm.

Thomasina did not order anything. She told me that she had been eating snack foods because it was all she could afford. At the lunch table, she opened her backpack and took out a bag of crackers. I told her to order something from the menu, and that I would pay. She ate like it was her last meal, and it was evident to me that she was not only exhausted from the walk, but not eating enough to sustain her energy to walk so much every day.

After we finished lunch, we stood up to leave, and Thomasina's legs buckled under her. She didn't fall, but she definitely was not steady on her feet. As she tried to walk, she winced in pain.

"Why don't you take a cab?" I suggested, holding out an arm to help her if needed.

She shook her head. "No money."

"I'll pay for it, don't worry."

But Thomasina insisted that if she agreed, I would have to take the cab with her. Now I felt a little unsteady. Take a cab? I had moved past that, right? I had overcome that "weakness" and shame, right?

Sensing my hesitance, Thomasina urged me to go on without her, and that she would be okay. "Seguire la corrente," she reassured me.

But I couldn't do it. I couldn't leave her behind. My "corrente," my flow, was not to leave others behind. "Corrente" comes from the Latin word "current," meaning "running." I was not running away any more. I was facing my fears and letting go of the voice in my head. "If you don't know where you want to go, then, it doesn't matter which path you take," said the Cheshire Cat to Alice when she was lost. Well, I knew my intentions and where I wanted to go. My intention was kindness, compassion, love, understanding, forgiveness, joy...living in Spirit and my True Self. And that is where I was walking—or at least, taking a cab.

As I settled in for bed that night, fresh from the cab ride, I couldn't help but think more about Thomasina's tattoo. The meaning of the Cheshire Cat is probably one of the most debated of all of the characters in *Alice in Wonderland*. Some see him as friendly, some as diabolical. Was that Lewis Carroll's purpose behind the cat? Does he represent the shadow and light side of us all...the good and the bad? Who we really are and who we pretend to be? The crazy in us and the sane, as perceived by others? Some critics say that the Cheshire Cat is the only one in the story who admits he is crazy, and with pride. Is that the True Self? I had always perceived the Cheshire Cat not as funny, but as someone not to be trusted. The passive-aggressive person who smiles to your face and tells you nice things, only to get what they want and are not at all interested in what you want or need. Or, if they don't get what they want from you, they attack you verbally, to your face, or worse, behind your back through gossip. They tell a tall tale of what a bad person you are, and other people believe that. *But that's not who I really am!*

"A rose is still a rose, even if hidden under different petals," said the Cheshire Cat as well. And, "I'm not crazy, my reality is just different from yours."

I was afraid of the Cheshire Cats in my life, and I wanted to run away from them and the pain they caused. My reality was that I was always sensitive and different from others. Walking my own path should have been a source of inspiration and pride. Instead, it had been a wellspring of shame and disgrace, isolation and disconnection. Was I the crazy, weird one because I wandered and wondered my way through life? I didn't think the way others did.

For the first time in my life, I was learning that I am free to be me through my heart, and spirit is the current that carries me back home, to me, my authentic self. "Follow your bliss, and the Universe will open doors where there were only walls."

> *"Would you tell me, please, which way I ought to go from here?"*
>
> *"That depends a good deal on where you want to get to," said the Cat.*
>
> *"I don't much care where—" said Alice.*
>
> *"Then it doesn't matter which way you go," said the Cat.*
>
> *"—so long as I get somewhere," Alice added as an explanation.*
>
> *"Oh, you're sure to do that," said the Cat, "if you only walk long enough."*

24

Lessons learned

24.1 Personal Reflection Activity

Gather five rocks. On each one, write an emotion or challenge that you feel is holding you back or holding you down. Go to a stream, river, lake, or the ocean and throw each rock into the water, while saying, "I let go of _____." How do you feel now?

24.2 Interpersonal Connection Activity

Play the board game "Life" with a partner. What are some of life's obstacles, challenges, triumphs, and detours? What are some possible solutions, workarounds, or new mindsets that can help move us along and progress through the game of Life?

25

BEING (A) PRESENT

*"Presence allows a deeper sense of identity. As Presence arises
you'll find in many areas of your life enormous improvements.
One is that the voice in the head that before created such
anguish and unhappiness no longer has that power over you.
As the mind's conditioning begins to subside, you can be with
people, events, and situations in a non-dysfunctional way,
aligned with whatever arises in the present moment."*

—ECKHART TOLLE, SPIRITUAL TEACHER

AFFIRMATION:

*I am present unto my true self and
therefore, a present unto the world.*

Now that I am in Galicia, the scenery and the experience
are so different. Is it because of the magical, mystical Celtic
atmosphere that surrounds me, or the cool temperature? The
smell of eucalyptus trees that permeates the air? Eucalyptus is
known for its healing ability to purify and clear away negative
energy. In Galicia, there is much controversy over the eucalyptus
tree here, as it's not native and was brought in by the Romans
centuries ago. It is considered by many to be an invasive tree
that depletes the soil and, as its leaves fall to the ground, changes
the ecosystem that surrounds it. I appreciate and respect this
perspective. I have another, which is just my experience as I pass
through the eucalyptus forests of Galicia.

They say that the journey on the Camino is divided into three phases: Body, Mind and Spirit. As pilgrims, we first struggle with the Body, and all the blisters and pains associated with our lives in the physical realm. Then, as those begin to heal, we struggle through the wounds and sufferings of our minds. The things we "make believe," the surreal and subjunctive doubts. Then, as we work through the Body and Mind, we finally arrive at spirit and Spirit. We have healed enough wounds and discovered enough about who we are and what has been holding us back. We arrive at that magical and mystical "lost" part of ourselves, only to discover what is real and who is real. What really matters, who really matters.

But most importantly, we arrive at the highest phase of our learning journey, the part that can create new possibilities because we have passed through remembering our past, understanding it, and applying it onto our future only to return to the present and its gift of infinite possibilities. We are discovering answers to the "whys" in our lives. When we start from where we are, here and now, and create from that point, THAT is the best lesson plan we could possibly create for ourselves and our lives. Like the eucalyptus, the false self is not native to who we really are. Yet we allow it to grow prolifically in our souls for some big payoff, even as it slowly depletes our soil and changes our ecosystem. At the same time, this process is an essential one, in order for us to learn what is important and what is not, so that we can find our way back to who we really are and what we really stand for. It is essential to the healing of our souls.

As I walk, it is cool and misting—or raining outright—much of the time. There are many forests and tree canopies that shelter pilgrims on the path, creating an almost enchanted experience. Mother Nature has truly worked her magic here, and the energy is light and uplifting despite the rain. In my reverie, I almost see the rain as the water from Heaven, cleansing and baptizing pilgrims as they finish their journey of self-discovery from the Body to the

Mind to the Spirit. A journey of rebirth and anointed blessing of the True Self. What could be more sacred than that?

The walks are around 18-20 kilometers per day, but they seem effortless and the experience is so different for me now. It is as if I am walking on clouds of joy, stopping to rest, take my socks off and give my feet much needed air. I sit in the grass and close my eyes and there is quiet, peaceful solitude, even though there are many pilgrims around me. I am taking pictures of almost every gift from Mother Nature that I see. This plant, that flower, a cow, a tree, a spiderweb. I stop and pick fruit from the apple and pear trees that are prolific in this area. I talk to the locals and learn more about what it is like to be a gallego (a person from Galicia) and to live in this beautiful yet challenging environment. Like with the eucalyptus trees, there is another perspective to the beauty of this pastoral farmland.

About five days out from Santiago, I came upon a lady who was sitting on a tree stump. She was a very large woman, about 300 pounds or so, and she was wiping her face with a towel and breathing heavily.

I stopped and asked her if she was okay. She said, "Yes, I just need to catch my breath and rest a minute."

I introduced myself. She told me that her name was Angie and that she was from Seattle. Before long, she got up and started walking again.

"Can I join you?"

She eyed me. "Yes, but... I'm really slow. I would just hold you back."

I chuckled. "I'm slow too. I welcome walking with someone who isn't going to rush me!"

So we set off together at our own pace. As we walked, I

noticed that every step Angie took seemed to require a great effort. She was breathing heavily, and stopped every five minutes or so to rest. Other pilgrims became impatient to pass her and some even made rude comments to her. With the helpfulness of multilingualism, I eavesdropped on a few conversations of groups of pilgrims walking together who said things like, "Oh my gosh, why is she here?" and "She'll never make it," and "Look at how fat she is!" or "Who does she think she is, trying to walk the Camino in her condition?" Some giggled, pointed or even laughed out loud as they passed her.

Needless to say, I was shocked and appalled. Weren't pilgrims on a spiritual or religious journey? What would these people say when they arrived at the Pilgrim's Office in Santiago and answer that question? That is not behavior from the Spirit, or any God of the world's wisdom traditions. The Pilgrim's Office also would ask what we learned from our journey on the Camino. What would they say?

Maybe: "I won."

Or: "I walked faster, farther, better than everyone else."

Or even: "I got drunk and lost my shoes. I partied in Spain on my birthday."

Possibly: "I checked another one off my bucket list, what's next?"

Or: "I did that thing in Spain that they did in that movie with Martin Sheen."

Or: "I hung out with my friends in Spain."

It all seemed to me like the shadow side of humanity raising its ugly head. How could they be so out of touch with the Spirit of the Camino? Even more, how could they be so cruel and insensitive to someone they didn't even know? They had no idea the journey Angie had been on, yet they were willing to judge her, compare themselves, and look down on her.

Walking with Angie, I was fortunate to hear about the journey she had been on, and it only increased my appalled reaction to the unkind passersby.

Angie described herself as a "different" child growing up. Different from other kids because she liked to read and make believe that she was a character in a story she was reading. At school, she often sat by herself and read while others played on the playground. Soon, other children noticed her being "different" and began to make fun of her and deliberately exclude her and bully her. She turned to food for solace, and began to put on weight. The more weight she put on, the more she was made fun of and the more she was made fun of, the more she turned to food for comfort.

I could tell that Angie was a sensitive flower in God's garden here on Earth, and as such, she took in so much pain and suffering. It was no surprise that she became a nurse to try to literally heal the pains and wounds of others, hoping that it would also heal her wounds. Oh, how I could relate to that! She married and had two children, and continued her nursing career. She also continued turning to food to comfort those wounds from childhood until she got so large that the hospital dismissed her, saying that she was too large and not physically fit to be able to handle the patients.

So Angie became a home healthcare nurse, but again, many people would not hire her because of her size, whether it was because they were disgusted and repulsed by it or they were afraid she was not competent because of it. The part of her story that broke my heart the most was when she talked about how her own two children had become "fed up" and "angry" with her that she "had let herself get so fat" and that she "didn't have enough willpower to stop eating and go on a diet." Then, one night, as she was eating a carton of ice cream and watching TV, the movie

The Way came on. She watched it and thought about how she had always wanted to travel, but she didn't because of her size. She ran away from life and the people in it and hid away in silence and solitude with her wounds and her pain. She didn't want to bother anyone or put them out and just lived life according to the comfort of others.

It was at that moment that Angie realized that her life was not her own, and that she had lost a part of herself many years ago due to the bullying she received. In the movie *The Way*, she watched the pilgrims somehow find that part of themselves again and "get their lives back." She wanted to do the same. So she managed to find work, and did double shifts for a year to save enough money to make the trip. She had started in St. Jean at the French border, like the pilgrims in the movie. However, the first day out in the Pyrenees, she realized that those mountains were too big and dangerous and that she would never make it if she started there. So she took a bus to Sarria, which is the required beginning point for the minimum amount to walk in order to receive your compostela in Santiago. By the time I met her, she had been walking about a week. I don't know how I hadn't passed her or noticed her before, except that she only walked about three or four hours a day, and then, would stop at an albergue for the night to rest.

"An albergue? Wow! How is that?" I asked, admiring her commitment. I hadn't had the nerve to stay in albergues, opting instead for the creature comforts of hotels.

Angie shrugged. "I deliberately chose to stay in albergues so that I would have to interact with the other people there."

I audibly gasped in response to this, followed by a shocked "*Why?*" which may have had a tone of judgment that really said, regrettably, "*Are you crazy?*" I wasn't being mindful; I was only reacting. I couldn't understand why she would willingly subject herself to cruelty, and my words came from a place of wanting to protect her. Nonetheless, I felt the heat of shame on my face.

She explained that she had been running away and hiding from people all her life, and that now was the time to face all their judgments and criticisms. To her, she needed to learn how to deal with them. She told me about how the first night on the Camino, she stayed in an albergue where she was put in a room with a German couple. Well, she snored quite loudly, and in the middle of the night, she was jarred awake by the couple literally trying to drag her out of bed, yelling at her in German. She told me, "I don't speak German, and I didn't know what the words meant, but I knew the tone and felt the familiar anger and shame."

She talked about how she tried to talk to other pilgrims in the albergues, and how many were polite, but also curt in their conversations and avoided eye contact. Some would even sit on the other side of the dining area away from her. She said it reminded her of school.

The entire time we were talking and walking, we would stop every five to ten minutes for her to rest, and Angie would say, "I know I am slow and holding you back, so feel free to go on ahead without me." Yet, it seemed to me that what she wanted more than anything was to be with another person on this journey, and no one had bothered to fulfill that. The Camino is a place where you can walk with others and share stories of life. Angie wanted that experience. She wanted to heal her wounds and make connections to others and help them heal their wounds too. But she was always left behind, and so she felt she could never move ahead. Others had abandoned and rejected her, and thus she did the same to herself.

This sensitive flower had not received the essential nurturing sunshine and water in her life to be able to grow and blossom. She had wilted under the repression and repulsion of others, and retreated and buried herself in the darkness of the dirt from which she came.

I couldn't help but see similarities in Angie's expectations of the Camino journey and my own. Is this the life journey for all of us? We struggle, retreat into the ever-nurturing soil of our souls, germinate and re-emerge to flower again. Is the key to be like a perennial, not an annual? Or is this ashes to ashes, dust to dust? Do we burn to cinder and rise again, like the Phoenix? Or perhaps we are always just part of an infinite Divine; a ray of light that extends in all directions; stardust.

That night as I pulled the blankets over me in my comfortable hotel bed, I thought of Angie in her albergue. Her story resonated with me, because I could see so many other stories reflected in it—my own story, the stories of so many students I had taught over the years.

"I am not enough."

"I am not lovable."

"I don't matter."

We all have experiences where we're made fun of, we feel like we're unloved, we don't belong, or we don't fit in. It is part of being human, yet instead of acknowledging these feelings as being "okay" and talking about them, we wrap them in shame and put a big bow of "not enough" on them, and we gift them to others through unkindness and lack of compassion. These feelings start in our childhood and continue into adulthood, and they don't all happen at home. They can originate in school and other public venues. Bullying is out of control in schools and in social media, with children and adults alike. These feelings of not-enoughness and not belonging are playing out in the classroom, in the home, in public places, in the media, and on the internet every day. They are not true feelings of the heart, but rather, made up stories in the mind that have been conjured up from the deepest, darkest places.

The journey of the Spirit brings us back to who we really are.

We learn from the Body and the Mind what creates the darkness in our lives, so that we can bring forth the Divine light from within us to guide us, protect us, and lead us to bliss. This is our True Self, and the authentic power of I AM.

I am enough.

I am lovable.

I do matter.

This is what we should be looking for and nurturing in children. Teachers and adults are luceras, guiding children on their learning journey to find their True Selves, what is real and important, and the will to help others along the way. This is our calling and our service to humanity. This is what put me in the classroom so many years ago, and what I felt I lacked when I left the classroom, got my spirit broken, and retired from the profession. This lost-ness is what put me on the Camino, and this one-ness is what I have been working my way back to.

Ashes to ashes, stardust to stardust.

25

Lessons learned

25.1 Personal Reflection Activity

Draw a picture of a creature or concept that protects you from negative thinking. How does this image help reflect who you truly are? Then, draw a picture of a creature or concept that protects you from being hurt by others. How does this creature operate— what does it do and when does it show up?

25.2 Interpersonal Connection Activity

Think of someone in your life who is struggling with something. You could also choose someone you don't personally know, or a fictional character. If you could give them one thing to help relieve their suffering, what would it be and why? Draw a picture of it or find a picture that represents that and give it to that person with a one-word "caption" or "title" that sums it all up for them. (Example: a picture of a big heart with the word "COURAGE" written across it)

26

THE MAGIC NUMBER THREE

"With peaks of joy and valleys of heartache, life is a roller coaster ride, the rise and fall of which defines our journey. It is both exciting and scary at the same time."

—SEBASTIAN COLE, AUTHOR

AFFIRMATION:

I trust that all is well and have faith that there is something of great value for me to learn from every experience that I have.

Finally, at long last, my rhythm on the Camino had fallen into a gentle, peaceful walk living completely in the present moment. The tune and lyrics of Louis Armstrong's song flowed through me...yes, what a wonderful world. I walked at my own pace and stopped when I felt like it. Every cell in my body seemed to be alive. I was taking in all the sensations of the world around me: I stopped to marvel at intricately woven spider webs glistening with dew in the morning sunlight; I stopped to take pictures of the twisted, massive trees that lined parts of the path. I stopped to breathe in the smell of the eucalyptus trees that were also a part of the dance of Mother Nature that was happening all around me. I stopped to take off my socks and sandals and soak in the cool water of a stream floating by. I stopped to pick apples off the trees and have lighthearted conversations with the many cows that were everywhere now, as dairy farming is a prime industry in the Galician region of Spain. I asked the cows, "Cómo estás hoy?" (how are you today?) to which the answer was always "MOO-ey bien"... a joke I liked to use on my students! It still made me chuckle every time. My spirit was light and so were my steps. It was like I was floating on air. I was in the state of what Joseph Campbell calls "bliss." Everything was alive, and so was I. No problems, no burdens, no incessant chatter in my head, no fear.

Even when I was in the classroom, I believed in the "magic" power of the number 3. Religious roots, perhaps. The power of the Trinity. The body, mind and spirit. The old saying that good (and bad?) things come in threes. Not sure, but I definitely passed it on to my students. They knew how I felt about the magical power behind "el número tres."

Three days out from Santiago, the path into my overnight town was not clearly marked with yellow arrows. It seemed to twist and turn more than what I had experienced before in other towns. At one point, it turned into a wooded area again, which seemed more like a winding maze. I even thought I caught a glimpse of other people ahead of me, but I couldn't tell if it was just my imagination. Suddenly I felt disoriented, struggling to figure out which way to go. What would lead me to the town and civilization, and not deeper into the woods to a point of no return?

Fear had not visited me for several days now, but it rushed right in again—without knocking and without an invitation. I retraced my steps to see if I had missed a yellow arrow. I tried to use the GPS on my phone, but there was no signal. It would be dark soon, and I didn't want to spend the night in the woods, alone and unprepared and lost without hope. "What had happened to those feelings of being 'alive?'" A nasty voice in my brain whispered to me. "Where is your bliss now, huh?"

I tried to quiet the voice and stay calm. I had been lost before and had found my way back. I could do the same thing again. But after about two hours of "wandering," I started to panic. It was then that I finally emerged onto a path, crossing a bridge over a little creek on the edge of a row of houses. From a maze of trees and bushes to a maze of buildings and concrete. And people... thank God! I was still lost, but at least I wasn't alone.

"I can figure this out," I said over and over to myself, hoping for the Kind Voice to be louder than the Mean Voice. I stopped in a bar to ask for directions, which seemed promising, but as soon as I tried to follow them, I realized they had left out key details. They clearly knew the way and had been there before, so their directions came in the form of, "The blah-blah-blah shop/bar/monument/house...you know which one I'm talking about, right?" But of course I didn't! I had never been there before, and I was *lost*.

All the while, it was getting darker. If I couldn't find my way in the daylight, how would I ever find it in the dark? Waves of fear and frustration were starting to pulse through my veins again. I felt the sensation you have when you are about to throw up: sweating, an aching stomach, my throat closing up. Everything was rushing to my head again, and there was a sense of "aliveness" to it, but not in a peaceful, good way.

I noticed a young lady with a backpack wandering around, just like I was. Our paths had crossed a couple of times, so finally, I asked her if she could speak Spanish and could help me. She was from Barcelona, and of course, had no problem with the language. It turns out she was looking for the same hotel as I was, and also like me, had been lost and confused in the woods. She had also stopped and asked for directions, but still could not find her way either. *Whew, I was not alone!* I was not stupid, incompetent, helpless or any of the other string of adjectives that had been free falling in my brain like paratroopers landing behind enemy lines of war.

The other lady and I put together our understanding of the

directions given to us, and soon figured out how to get there. When I arrived at the hotel, the Canadian sisters were there, worried that I been lost and wouldn't make it. They invited me to dinner, but I remembered the last time I had dinner with them in the aftermath of a fear storm, and quietly excused myself to my room. I wanted to quietly and calmly process what had just happened, and how discordant it had felt to the "wonderful world" I had been living during the day.

I thought I had "mastered" this walking thing on the Camino, and here I was again feeling like I did the first three days out. How could I have gotten lost? How could I have let my mind and the shadow side of me take over like that again? Had I not learned anything? Why couldn't I look at it as a setback instead of a defeat or a failure? Needless to say, it was a sleepless night of wandering in my thoughts, feeling as lost, afraid, and hopeless as I had felt earlier that day.

The next morning, I met the Canadian sisters for breakfast. They announced that they had decided to walk with me the whole day as it was a shorter distance than normal and that they would have no problem slowing down to my pace and still make it to the next destination. They also added that I probably would welcome their company, as though to assure me that I wouldn't be alone with the possibility of getting lost again. Of course, all of this was presented with the intention of being helpful and caring, I'm sure, but I struggled being on the receiving end of it. The "help" feels like you're being told, "I'm being a nice person, and oh by the way, I am better at these things than you are." It made me feel like a child, or a helpless damsel being rescued. Perhaps it felt a little Cheshire Cat-like.

I should have graciously declined, but I didn't. I guess I didn't want to hurt their feelings. But truthfully, there were so many complicated emotions permeating that decision to agree to walk with them. There was, of course, the fear of being lost again, and the feeling of being helpless and hopeless and not enough. But there was also the feeling of being "honored" that they finally wanted to accept me into their exclusive and seemingly competent walking club—and, miraculously, just by association, I too would be competent and free of the struggles I had been experiencing. Hah! My illusions were delusions.

As we walked, the path passed through forests and gentle rolling hills full of orchards and cows. It was cool. The sun was shining. It was lovely. The feeling of bliss was gently rolling over me again, like the fog that caressed the trees in the forest. So magical. Susan would stop every once in a while and ask to take a picture of me on the Camino, which I was immensely grateful for. I didn't have many pictures of just me, and it was sweet of her to offer. She walked beside me as we chatted, talking about family, travel and life in general.

Joan, as you may have guessed, was a different story. She still walked way ahead of us, turning around every once in a while with a frown, or a gesture of impatience and exasperation. When she did walk with us, she grilled me about my knowledge of Spain, and Europe in general. She asked detailed questions about history or geography or the politics of particular regions, some of which I knew, and some of which I didn't. When I said, "I don't know," or "I'm not sure," she would follow up with, "Hm. I thought you would know that." Or, she would pick a certain word or detail I had communicated, and argue about the validity of it. "Really? Well, I doubt that," or "Hm, I find that hard to believe." In spite of all of Susan's kindness and the beautiful nature surrounding us, I started to feel triggered by Joan's behavior. It seemed like she was baiting me, just trying to engage in a negative exchange of energy. In return, I was armoring up more and more.

It was such a familiar feeling that I had struggled with all my life. Why did it seem to continually happen to me? Why did I feel triggered by such behavior? Did I come across as a "know-it-all" to others? I didn't mean to. I just love learning, and sharing my enthusiasm and curiosity about things I learn. Maybe it was taking the teacher part of me too far. But over time, I have come to realize that we are all teachers. As humans, we love to connect to others through knowledge and experiences that we package and deliver as stories. We begin our connections with phrases like, "Did you know/see/read/hear...?" or "I just saw/read/heard the other day..."

What happens after that can go many ways depending on the perceived intentions of the two interlocutors. That's when the information gets filtered through our brain's perception of past experiences, knowledge, and feelings, not to mention our future projections of the same. There was something going on with Joan and her perceived perception of me as a threat. As a result of her behavior, I was trying to prove to her that I wasn't this person she was trying to make me out to be through her comments and reactions. I wanted to make clear that I was not weak or dumb or incompetent. With Susan, our interactions didn't communicate that message. I felt accepted and validated by her. With Joan, I felt constantly attacked and invalidated.

This was a dance I had done before. I've been a people-pleaser my whole life, to the point where years ago I bought the book *The Disease to Please* by Harriet B. Braiker. Was it my Ego? I had read everything that I could about the Ego, yet here I was again, struggling with myself and my relationship with another person. I didn't want conflict. I just wanted to get along. I just wanted peace with others and, most of all, peace within me. I had been seeking that my whole life. I thought I had finally found the solution to the problem and got the answer right. I had passed that test and learned the lesson. I was done with learning about that, right? Just like a lesson in a book. I've covered the material in Chapter 1, page after page. Check! Now it's done, I've taken the test, and passed with an A. Check! I've mastered the concept. I can move on to something new in Chapter 2 and never revisit

Chapter 1 again. Oh, the learning journey couldn't be further from this pattern. Life just doesn't really work that way. After all, today I was living proof that if you get lost once on your journey, it doesn't mean you'll never get lost again.

In the classroom, I had an easier time embracing this reality. I understood that my students needed multiple opportunities to learn what I wanted them to learn. I knew that each child's journey in learning was different, and very personal to them based on their experiences, likes and dislikes, personality, hopes and dreams, etc. I was confident in the knowledge that there was a "bigger picture" lesson, and that the textbook wasn't the curriculum or the "magic pill" that was going to deliver the prescribed remedy to ignorance as set by some higher-up government standards. As a person in the classroom, it was easier for me to lead with my heart. My students knew that, and embraced me. I was vulnerable and loved my students unconditionally. Did I have conflict? Sometimes. But I tried to stay focused on the light within them and the light within me. The light of pure and innocent love. To be honest, I had always felt pretty successful in this goal. But as a person outside the classroom... I struggled in this pursuit. I shielded my heart from all potential pain and suffering. I only felt safe with certain people to let my light shine through and their light shine on me.

As it was a shorter day, we arrived at our hotel around mid-afternoon. It was a straight shot. No twists or turns. Clearly marked yellow arrows. The three of us agreed to clean up, rest a little and then meet for dinner. We had a typical Pilgrim's meal: caldo gallego, delicious hot bread, salad, chicken, and red wine. The company continued much the same way as it had during the day—Susan pleasant, and Joan demanding.

We parted ways after the meal, turning in a little earlier than usual, and agreed to meet at 7:00 am for breakfast. About an hour after I had fallen asleep, I was suddenly and violently awakened by a sharp pain in my stomach, like someone had reached into my mid-section and was trying to yank my stomach out of my body. I had never felt anything like it before. I bolted up in bed, not sure what was going on. Then, over the next six hours, it was as if I was giving birth to my stomach. I experienced wave after wave of slow and painful contractions until dawn.

I have had the flu many times in my life. I have had food poisoning several times as well. I wanted to believe that this was either the flu or food poisoning, but it felt different. It was like nothing else I had experienced before. Later, I came to realize that I was releasing all the poison from my solar plexus—the seat of my power, in Chakra terms. I was cleansing my gut and making way for my intuition to take over and guide me. It was like my body was ridding itself of everything "bad" that was making me sick…everything that I had swallowed and choked down all my life. All of the experiences when I gave up my power to others and did not stand in my truth and shine my light in the world. It was making a clear path, not from my stomach, but from my heart. A path for my voice of truth and light to come out. It was a detox of the soul. A release of all of the pain bodies and festering wounds that I had allowed to live inside me for so long. I had kept them alive with my fears, doubts, anger, resentments, and victimhood. It was time to let them go.

Of course, it didn't feel like that at the time. At our 7:00 am meet-up, I staggered downstairs to tell Joan and Susan that I had been up all night "sick" and that I wasn't going to be able to walk with them.

"Oh no, I'm so sorry!" Susan exclaimed.

"Sick, what kind of sick?" Joan immediately zeroed in on the details. "Vomiting? But we ate the same thing all day, and neither one of us was sick. That doesn't make sense…" It seemed like Joan thought I was making it all up just to get out of walking with them.

Regardless, I went back to my room and slept for a couple of hours until the maid service knocked on the door and asked when I was leaving. Feebly, I gathered my things and went downstairs. My stomach muscles felt like I had done a million sit-ups, and I didn't feel like eating or drinking anything. Other than that, I felt okay. So, why not walk? What else was I going to do? So, I started walking…in the rain, no less.

I'll pause here for all the gasps of shock, moans of disapproval. Feel free to shout, "You fool!" Yes, it was a foolish thing to do. After a couple of hours, I was feeling weak…very weak. I was lightheaded, and it felt like I was in a vacuum with everything moving in slow motion. I was starting to hallucinate. The path swam before me as I struggled to plant one foot in front of the other. I staggered a few steps, and then, down I went.

I had passed out in the middle of a cow pasture.

The good news was that I didn't fall in cow poo! The bad news was that I couldn't get up. I was too weak. I was dehydrated. Since I had left later than all the other pilgrims, I was all alone on the Camino. I had fallen, I couldn't get up, and there was no one around to help me. No cell signal either. I was surely going to die, and they would find my dried up body in a cow pasture looking like all the cow paddies. Even through my dulled senses, this was the most scared I had ever been in my life. A voice inside me said, *pray!*

"God, I did a stupid thing, and I need your help! I shouldn't have tried to walk today. I should have taken a cab. What was I thinking? Please, God? Please, por favor? Send me a cab. I don't care if I'm not a true peregrina. Send me a cab. I don't want my obituary to say, '*She died in Spain in a cow pasture because she wouldn't take a cab. Killed by her Pride and Ego.*'"

Why didn't I literally listen to my gut and go with that message to take it easy and be gentle with myself?! What was I trying to prove with such a foolish decision? WHO was making that choice?

Then I thought about my family, especially my daughters. I started weeping and, ironically, begging God to send me a cab. "God, please, I want to see my family again. I still have so much to do, to give back to the world. This is not it for me!"

I have no idea how long this went on, but all of a sudden, I looked up, and there it was. My miracle. A cab, right here in the middle of the cow pasture.

A man flung open the cab door and said, "Señora, necesita ayuda?" *Ma'am, do you need help?*

His voice was like a chorus of angels. I crawled into the cab and told him the name of my hotel. He asked what happened to me, and I told him. He said his name was Luis and he would help me. True to his word, when we arrived at the hotel, he got out of the cab and guided me into the hotel. My room was not ready yet, so they told me to wait in the bar area. Luis helped me over to the bar and told the bartender to bring me an Aquarius, citrus flavor. Aquarius is similar to a sports drink to replenish electrolytes.

Luis sat and chatted with me for about an hour. He wouldn't let me give him money for the fare, nor for the Aquarius. Then when I started to look a little better, he told the bartender to take care of me, and he left. He really was like an angel, literally appearing out of nowhere in my time of need to answer my pleas. Now he was gone, and I would never see him again. And yet, he had saved me. Who knows what would have happened to me if Luis hadn't shown up at the exact moment that he did.

I should be indebted to him for the rest of my life. But kindness and other acts of humanity do not have faces, nor do they go on a scorecard. They cannot be measured, calculated, timed, or standardized. They come from the heart and forever touch our lives. This was what I had seen on the Camino over and over. Lucero/a after lucero/a, lighting flames of all kinds and guiding those in need, in whatever way they needed. This was the medicine that I had needed to heal my soul. Faith, humanity, and hope were the Trinity that had restored my spirit and made me whole again. They are the fuel that keeps us alive and on the path to our True Self.

The bartender, Carlos, was from Cuba; he had come to Spain to do the Camino too. Like so many other luceros/as I'd encountered, he was so transformed by his experience and touched by the connection he felt with Spanish culture, he had decided to stay and work there. I have known many people from Latin America who said that they felt like they were "home" when visiting Spain. Even though the colonial roots of their ancestry yield complicated implications and mixed feelings, there's still the undeniable sense of familiarity in the smell of strong coffee in the afternoon, the mannerisms of the people, the strong bonds of family values, the gathering of everyone from all age groups together in the plaza to connect, chat, and solve the world's problems. Some of them have shared with me that it was like an unearthing— exploring and connecting to a part of themselves that they did not know, or had forgotten was there. In a way, this is what I had discovered on my journey on the Camino, but not with the culture and people outside of me. I had finally unearthed, explored and re-connected to that essential, true Me. The root of my Self's spiritual existence...the essence of my being...the connection to my humanity and the light within.

As soon as my room was ready, Carlos helped carry my bags to my room. Throughout the day, he checked on me a few times to bring me more Aquarius and make sure I was okay. Was he just a bartender, or in fact another angel sent to restore my faith in humanity and give me hope? Is each and every one of us an angel with a similar mission, but we just have not unearthed, explored or connected to that Higher purpose in life? Is there not a Greater Good that we can all bear the light of?

I slept and drank my Aquarius the rest of the afternoon until sunrise the next day. The last day to walk into Santiago. I would finally make it to my destination. I couldn't tell if my stomach was hurting from the events of the night before, or if I had nervous energy racing through my body in anticipation of finally finishing my journey. With the sun peeking over the horizon behind me, I meditated to try to calm everything down and set my intention for the day. I had another Aquarius, and Carlos gave me "one for the road," as I thanked him profusely for his care.

Then, I set off on the final stage of the Camino into Santiago de Compostela. Joan and Susan had stayed at a different hotel so they were nowhere in sight. Everyone else I had met along the way was somewhere other than where I was...some ahead, some behind, and some had left all together.

I was completely on my own, and I was perfectly okay with that. I didn't feel alone though. I felt like there was someone with me now that was my best friend, my soulmate, my teacher, my spiritual guide. Someone who would always be there for me and never let me down. A person whom I could trust and feel safe with. A person who loved me no matter what and expected nothing in return. A person who listened with an open heart, understood everything about me and accepted me for who I was...complete and profound unconditional love.

This person was me. My True Self, my Divine Guiding Angel Spirit, from whom I could never truly be lost. To whom I could always find my way back. Whom I could always trust to never lead me off my true path.

26

Lessons learned

26.1 Personal Reflection Activity

Think of a time when you felt powerless and write down the details to answer the WWWWWH about the situation and how you felt. Take each detail describing the situation and place that sentence or those words into the appropriate drawing below... trash or treasure?

26.2 Interpersonal Connection Activity

Based on what you've learned so far in your life experiences, create an acronym for GRACE for your life to model and teach others. Give a copy to someone for whom you would like to help "light the way."

G _____

R _____

A _____

C _____

E _____

27

THE WHOLE TRUTH

"Seek the wisdom that will untie your knot. Seek the path that demands your whole being."

—RUMI, POET & SCHOLAR

AFFIRMATION:

I seek truth in all that I am and all that I do so that I can feel whole (some).

The morning I would arrive in Santiago de Compostela, the last day of my Camino journey, I woke up in a paradoxical state of excited calm. With measured breaths, I read through the Pilgrim's Prayer given to me by Liliana. I pulled on the socks and sandals given to me by José Manuel and hoisted on my backpack, considerably lighter than when I began, both literally and metaphorically. I discarded my last empty bottle of Aquarius given to me by Carlos. I didn't see Joan and Susan at breakfast. And then, ready for the day, I stepped out of the hotel and onto the path.

The last day of walking would be about 20 kilometers, five to six hours walking (for me, with stops). I was present for every single step that I took. This was it, and I wanted to savor every second and moment of the experience. The feeling of bliss would be an understatement. It was like I was having an out-of-body experience. Every atom of my being was alive and taking in the experience. Time had seemed to slow down and my five senses had seemed to ramp up. It felt like the scene in a movie when the main character is running in slow motion to who or what ever they had been seeking throughout the entire story.

As I approached the plaza, my footsteps tracing along the paths of countless peregrinos before me, I could hear the sound of a gaeta being played. As I got closer to its source, its festive and lively rhythm evoked the feeling of a celebration. It also felt like the heralding of an annunciation: "I made it!" I stopped to take video of the man playing the gaeta and to savor the feeling of being so close to my "destination," what I believed, at the time, to be the "end" of my journey.

I progressed closer and closer to the Cathedral, the narrow streets getting more and more crowded, not just with pilgrims, but also with tourists. I rounded the corner on the street leading down into the plaza, as I had done so many times before as a student on my way to class, but this experience was so different now. I was still a student, though, I supposed. I couldn't have experienced the previous weeks' journey and *not* used the word *learning*.

I'd seen this view dozens of times before, but nothing could prepare me for the descent into the main plaza. It is purposefully constructed for dramatic effect: as you walk, your view opens up from the narrow street into the sprawling plaza, filled with people and the magnificent, massive Cathedral towering above you. It stops you in your tracks. Many pilgrims literally fall to their knees at this point, in a prayer of humility and gratitude. I was no exception. I fell to my knees and began to weep.

A kind British woman came over and offered to help me up and to take my picture, but I couldn't even speak. I was overwhelmed with emotion. It was like I was finally exhaling and relaxing after holding my breath for so long. A lifetime of emotion flooded out of me in a wave of relief. I felt like I was being lifted up onto the shoulders of hope again.

Incidentally, the word "relief" is originally from the Latin word "relevare," which means "to raise again." It encapsulated the exact feeling I felt. My soul had been raised up; my True Self once again revealed from the shadows. And now, a feeling of lightness, like I was freed from under the burdens that had held me down for so long. Lightness, as though all the dark had been cast out, and only the light in me, and the light of the world around me, were shining brightly. And then, an overwhelming feeling of love and peace and exuberance. With every step I took toward the Cathedral, I was awash with a warm, peaceful calm, and a growing feeling of excitement and exaltation.

As if on a cloud, I approached the entrance to the Cathedral, ready to follow the centuries-old traditions and rituals that celebrate this milestone along the Camino's way. Rituals that would also mark this milestone in my life and glorify it in my memory forever. Just as I had left stones along the Camino to literally mark the awakening and subsequent enlightening experiences of personal growth and learning, it was now time to celebrate this milestone in my life through several "rites of passage." Rites of passage are so important to celebrate our transformation. One could merely walk through the magnificent doors of the cathedral and walk around admiring the opulence and grandeur of the construction. However, like with any experience in life, it is certainly more meaningful and more enriched if you can make connections through knowledge and learning.

Once inside the Cathedral, the first thing the pilgrim sees is the Portico de la Gloria. This is the portal or gateway into the main part of the cathedral where the body of St. James lies. It used to be that pilgrims could enter these main doors, but now they are only used during a Holy Year when St. James's birthday falls on a Sunday. Pilgrims also used to be able to follow certain rituals at the Portico de la Gloria before entering the cathedral. But today, this part of the cathedral is closed to the public due to overuse and the desire to protect the physical structure. I did not realize that this part of the cathedral had become off-limits since the last time I was there 15 years earlier. I was so disappointed to not be able to actually conduct these meaningful rituals, so instead, I sat down in the part of the plaza facing the Pórtico de la Gloria and read about them in my Camino guidebook, closing my eyes and imagining myself performing them.

The first ritual takes place at the central pillar, called the Tree of Jesse, which has a seated St. James carrying a staff and a scroll that reads "The Lord sent Me." It is here that pilgrims used to place the fingers of their right hand into the five indentations on the marble and say a prayer of gratitude or five Hail Marys for their safe arrival. This is such a powerful reminder that gratitude is a guiding light in life. At the base of the Tree of Jesse are two crouching animals with their mouths wide open. In between is the bust of Maestro Mateo, the architect and creator of the Pórtico de la Gloria. It is here that a pilgrim places an arm in each mouth of the beast and bumps their head against that of Maestro Mateo, with the hope that his genius and creative talents will be imparted to you. Once entering the cathedral, pilgrims can walk up the stairs and behind the altar of the shrine to Santiago. The ritual here used to be that pilgrims would place their hat on the head of the statue of Santiago in exchange for his jeweled, golden crown of glory.

Probably the greatest and most famous ritual, that still exists to this day, is the Pilgrim's Mass in which the "botafumeiro," a very large, ornate, silver urn-like object filled with burning, smoking incense, is swung through the transept of the cathedral by eight tiraboleiros. This tradition began centuries ago in order to cover up the stench of the pilgrims who attended the Mass, as they had not bathed regularly. It was performed daily at noon. However, due to the economics of performing such a ritual, now it is only done when 300 euros is collected to cover the cost. I would return the next day for this ritual, but for today, I skipped it in favor of heading to the Oficina del peregrino to obtain my compostela.

The line at the Oficina del peregrino was quite long and literally filled with people from all "walks of life." Some were quietly standing in contemplation and reflection. Some were chatting animatedly and exchanging stories and photos of their experiences on the Camino. Some had traveled on foot, some on bicycle, and there were even two people who used wheelchairs.

I stood in line among all of them, waiting for my turn to "take the test" and receive my certificate of completion. I thought about all the pilgrims I had talked to before. When I was a student in Santiago, I had walked with pilgrims on this last stage of the Camino to listen to their stories and find out why they had taken the journey and what they had learned from it.

Now, I was the one walking that path, but not in their shoes. Each one had a unique experience and story to tell. There were some similarities, yes, but mostly, each pilgrim's journey was unique to who they were. Each one walked away with a greater understanding of who they were and their purpose in life. Each of us was walking home to our True Selves.

So of course, nothing was standardized. There was no checklist of pre-determined experiences to be fulfilled and checked off. I thought about my own learning experience on the Camino. It certainly wasn't about mastery, but rather about evolution. It wasn't important to check boxes; it was important to be curious and open to the discovery. It was about becoming aware of who I am, and the gifts I'm here to share with the world for the Greater Good. To grow into the greatest version of myself in order to help others and to help create a better world for all to live in. These are the real "tests" in life and they should be celebrated, not initiated and implemented to gather data, but rather to mark and make connections to our common humanity.

And yet, in order to receive my compostela, I just had to answer those three simple questions:

> *1. What is your name?*

> *2. Where are you from?*

> *3. What was your purpose for doing the Camino... spiritual or religious?*

My experiences on the Camino transcended any stamp, any certificate, any checkmark. How could I even begin to summarize them? They had melted away so much that was keeping me frozen in my life, keeping me from moving forward, moving up, moving on...just moving at all. When the extra "stuff" melted away, I was left with essential truths. Lessons that were meaningful to me because of my own context, my own experiences, my own learning. So many steps, so many missed-steps, so many opportunities, so many experiences, so many lessons.

> Life is a personalized learning journey of self-awareness and empowered choices.

> My path (i.e. learning experiences) is determined by my choices and my level of self-awareness.

> I am not perfect, but I am whole and not broken, and therefore, don't need to "fix" anything about myself (or others, for that matter!).

> I am a powerful, Divine creator of light and should not die with my song still inside me!

> I AM ENOUGH!

> I AM WORTHY!

> I am allowed to BE ME and BE REAL! No labels. Pure, unconditional love.

I must live from my AUTHENTIC power. Don't let others define me or determine my path.

The greatest power in the world can be found within and not in the people or things outside of us, and I will use this power for the greater good of all.

I MATTER, and so do others! We are all in this together.

I will live with an open heart and try to always be mindful of my intentions and my choices.

Relationships and human connections are important, but I can gracefully walk away from people and things that don't align with my True Self and my core beliefs.

We all just want to be validated and accepted and find our place to belong and feel safe. I need to recognize and honor that in me and in others.

I will live in Spirit and be "inspired" every day by gratitude, compassion, grace, kindness and love because they are the most important "main ideas" of life.

We are all seeking meaning to our lives and our purpose here on Earth.

We are all teachers and students living in a world classroom called humanity.

There is no perfection or A+, just a circle of continuous opportunities to practice.

Limiting beliefs about ourselves and others just hold us back and create pathways to the impossible, rather than guiding us along the path of the possible. My mantra is "Yes, I CAN!"

Meditation, intuition, mindfulness, prayer, faith and love are best practices of the heart that will always lead us to the "right" answer we are seeking.

Don't be afraid to be myself, to let my light shine and to sing the song in my heart because therein lie my purpose, my calling and my greatest gift to the world.

These are my own personal "stamps" in my own personal credencial of life. Yes, I have ink stamps in a paper document that showed my physical journey across Spain. But these lessons show the true importance of stamps on a journey: they are simply stops along the way where you can pause and reflect on the AHA moments and OH NO moments you experienced. Then, you keep going until your next opportunity to stop.

The greater understanding I had discovered was this: we are human. We don't have all the answers. We get lost. We fall down. We fail. We get back up, and we fall down again. Eventually all our paths literally dead end, but in the meantime, life is truly all about the journey and not the destination.

In the more specific context of my own life, I had lost my way. I was off path. I had so many questions and felt that I didn't have any answers. It was as if I had failed my life's multiple choice test. Once I retired from teaching, I didn't know who I was or what my purpose was anymore. My soul had been shattered into pieces, and I was looking for them on the Camino, with other searching pilgrims. We all lose our way, and many times over a lifetime.

And, as a teacher, I couldn't help but wonder: why are we not better preparing our children for those times when we are lost and don't have all the answers? How can we learn to let go of fear and become curious and open to the possibilities? What subjects and ideas need to "grace" the hallways and classrooms of our schools, to help us discover real truths and greater understandings about who we are and what our place is in this world? As luceras for our students, we need to re-imagine what enLIGHTenment looks like in our beloved profession.

Like Dorothy in *The Wizard of Oz*, my journey took me on an adventure to discover my True Self through experiences with my environment and the other people in it. My own feelings of "not enough" mirrored back at me through others who walked faster, prepared better, and trained more. I witnessed my own feelings of victimization and entitlement through the brothers and sisters I met along the way. I saw my own abusive self-talk and perceived failure through the 87-year-old woman who fell. Joan was a whole hall of mirrors, with her drive to meet arbitrary "standards" and impose them harshly on herself and others using aggression and arrogance. Through Christy, I saw myself always running and pushing myself to extremes by "jumping into the rabbit hole" like Alice's White Rabbit. But also through her, urged by Thomasina's tattoo, I saw myself fooled, learning not to trust any of the Cheshire Cats that showed up in my life.

My Ego, my fears, my "broken" pieces of darkness had reflected through these people and shown me my shadow side. But the truth was that I had not lost anything nor was anything broken. It was there all along. As Glinda the Witch says, "You've always had the power, my dear. You just had to learn it for yourself."

It's true; the goodness and light I've had all along was shown to me on my journey, too. There were the young people, Thomasina, and Victor, who embodied all of my students —and even me, as a language student. The Italian man who went out of his way and walked the 87-year-old woman back to town because it was the "right thing to do." Sandra, who followed her calling to be a "lucera," whose light touched and healed others. David, stripped down to his barest and most vulnerable essentials, and

Mary, the hospitalera, who both lived humble lives of service to others. The priest, Anthony, who showed me that listening with an open heart is the greatest gift I can give every day.

Even closer to my heart was Liliana, who showed me loving kindness, unconditional support, and a belief in my potential to do and to be exactly who I was meant to do and to be—something I prided myself on giving to my students, but couldn't seem to manage for myself. What gratitude I felt to Liliana for those gifts. Then there was the Blanco Family, José Francisco, Ofelia, and José Manuel, who showed me that unconditional love, grace, and joy was possible in families, and could be extended outside of the family, too. And finally, there was the part of me that I saw in Angie—the child who was "different" because she was "sensitive," and who was bullied. The child who felt like she didn't fit in or belong, even in her family, and who struggled to rise out of her circumstances and context, weighed down by the distrust borne from painful memories.

With more time, distance, and perspective now, I look back on how many things I did as a teacher that just "came naturally." So much that was borne from my heart and that inner child in me that so wanted to heal and be whole. One of my signature strategies for learning with my students was to tell them that they just needed to "follow the yellow brick road" and that they would get to the "Land of Ahhhhs." Their learning journey was just to be curious, explore, take risks and follow the signs to the next step. Like the Camino, I was leaving "yellow arrows" to show them the steps along the way, but that their learning journey would only be complete when they had reached that moment when they felt, and sometimes literally said, "ahhhhh" or "aha!" I GET IT! Enlightenment, the lightbulb switching on, an epiphany, a revelation or manifestation. An almost spiritual moment, in the sense of the awakening of the light in you to personally make a connection to the learning and grow from that learning. Follow the light within.

When I left the classroom and worked at the bureaucratic level of the local school district, my spirit suffered. Our educational institutions in the U.S. have become as scripted as medicines produced by Big Pharma. We just keep looking at the symptoms and not at the root causes of the "sickness" that is running rampant through our educational system. People need pathways, opportunities and loving support to make choices that are personally appropriate and beneficial for their journey in life. If not, then our human spirit suffers, and sickness sets in—as mine did. I see it happening to teachers and children every day in the classroom. And it just keeps getting worse!

My journey on the Camino cracked my heart wide open and cleared a path for the light of my Being to shine. It had cut through all the doubt, fear, anger and darkness and made way for the light of love and hope to flow once again and give me life. I had learned so much on my journey and re-discovered the inner child within me. I had found my way home to the place where that sweet, innocent, beautiful child lives. This place is called "Spirit," home of my True Self, and I never want to leave or live anywhere else again!

27

Lessons learned

27.1 Personal Reflection Activity

Think of three different occasions when you felt like you failed or you didn't feel like you were who you are, or like what you did was enough.

Describe the situation	What caused the feeling?
Effect on choices or behavior	What if...?

Describe the situation	What caused the feeling?
Effect on choices or behavior	What if...?

Describe the situation	What caused the feeling?
Effect on choices or behavior	What if...?

27.2 Interpersonal Connection Activity

Create a circle of 5-6 people. One person has a small ball or hacky sack that they will toss to someone else in the group while saying something kind to that person. Examples: "You're a really kind person," "You're really good at math." The person who catches the ball says "truth," and tosses the ball to another person, making a positive statement about them. Afterward, fill in the chart below.

Person in the circle	3 kind things heard

27.3 Bonus Lesson Activity

Fill in the circle of learning.

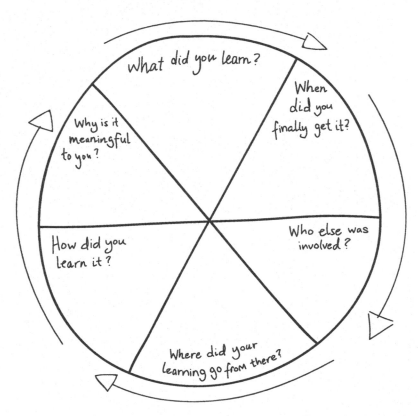

AFTERWORD

THE GIFTS OF LIFELONG LEARNING

"The greatest gifts are a portion of thyself."
—RALPH WALDO EMERSON, AUTHOR

AFFIRMATION:

I share my gifts with the world in order to inspire and light the way for others.

The lessons I learned on the Camino have forever changed me. After I returned, I felt as if I were floating on air. I was so in love with life and marveled at everything, just like when I was a child. I thought, "What a huge lesson to learn. I understand! I got this now!" AHA!

Like lessons in the classroom, it's easy to think that these lessons are a "one and done" deal. As soon as I "understand" them, then, I must have mastered them, right?

Not so. Knowledge and experience are not commodities or goods to be offered up as evidence of mastery. Nor are they weapons to be used to take down others on the field of battle of the Egos. "I got this, and I won't have to deal with Ego or fear or anything again." Once more, a big fat AHA!

Am I still triggered by some people like Joan? Yes! Am I still afraid of situations I find myself in that I feel I can't get out of? Yes! This is completely normal. But the lessons on the Camino have raised my awareness and given me something to which I can relate my new experience. I have the power to make a different choice of how I want it to manifest in my life based on my intentions and my vision of my True Self. I will never reach perfection. I can only become more proficient and professed in what I have learned.

As I muse more and more on what it means to learn and know, I find myself often returning to Maya Angelou's maxim "When you know better, you do better." "Knowing" to me now means awareness and empowering choices. It is not something served up on a silver platter for us to possess and covet. It is not something that can be memorized and measured through a finite number of choices that are "one size fits all." Knowing is not in the minute details that will be discreetly and randomly tested, but rather from the experiences and the feelings that we hold near and dear to our hearts and to the humanity in each of us. From every lesson, we raise our awareness of who we are and what our place in the world is. From that awareness or "knowing" we can make different choices. We are always vulnerable to "failure," but it is in our failures (our Faithful Attempts in Learning) that we have our greatest learning opportunities. And, our greatest strengths and courage can be discovered through our vulnerabilities. Our life lessons are just scaffolded and spiraled throughout our journey here on this Earth. That's "teacher speak" for step-by-step and multiple opportunities to "figure it out." It's really more like "knowing is empowering" instead of "knowledge is power."

What I truly know about learning is that it never ends until we take our last breath. We have and we need multiple opportunities to PRACTICE until we get better at it. But we never perfect anything! That is why we are human. All we can do is be lifelong learners, seekers and sharers of truth and light—luceros/as. We are all teachers and learners to one another through our experiences, our stories, our truths and our light.

Even if we have a compostela now and again, there is no multiple choice test, end-of-life exam, or pass/fail option. There is only now and what we can learn from this moment, from within ourselves and from each other. Then, we just have more choices and more opportunities to practice growth each day. Hopefully we become "just a little better today than we were yesterday," as Wayne Dyer puts it. As we chop the wood and carry the water, living in the present moment, like Eckhart Tolle says, we have the opportunity to discover, again and again, who we truly are. We have the chance to share our gifts with the world, to be whole and shine brightly, and to live our lives in the light. There's not just one chance, but multiple opportunities to figure out the answer that is personal to us. Many lessons, no real failures, no one right answer…we are each just creating the lyrics of our own personal song to sing to the world! Gift it with love!

So, I would like to end with a poem that I wrote as a gift to all children in the world, but especially to the child and the light within each of us that accompanies us each and every day on our journey through life. The light is always there, and you are always enough!

The Light Within

> Look, my child.
>
> At the light within you.
>
> It is your gift to this world.
>
> It is the hope for your future
>
> And for the well being of humanity.
>
> It is your superpower to make change
>
> To inspire, to guide, to illuminate
>
> The path that is uniquely yours

But that is also shared by all.

With this guiding light, you are your own hero in your life's journey

But also in the journey of others to help them discover

The light within.

See, my child

Your place in a world full of meaning through dreams, potential and possibilities.

Be curious, connect, communicate and create

From what is personally meaning-full

Until your cup runneth over

With love, joy, compassion, peace and wonder

That will shimmer and shine and radiate

The light within.

Taste, my child

The sweetness of life and the bitterness too

For we cannot know one without the other

Nor can we learn and grow without them both because

Reflection and a taste of "one's own medicine"

As seen through our interactions with others

Can lead us and guide us to profound truths of knowing

The light within.

Feel, my child.

The warm tingle in your tummy

That knows and glows and flows

Through you like a never-ending fountain of creativity

That will nourish and give life and inspire

But will also serve as a current to carry the good within us all

And to beckon the wayfarer in each one of us

To seek and find and share

The light within.

Listen, my child

To the whispers in your soul

To the Spirit in the wind

Let it all give you breath

To live, to do, to be

Through words of positivity

And actions filled with energy

That will create a stream of

Good in this world

A model for us all to follow and soon discover

The light within.

Speak, my child

Words of kindness and of affirmation

And the truth of greater understandings

Of a humanity, that, although may seem a dream

In a landscape of quixotic windmills of reality

It is never wasted time and there are never wasted words

Spent on the ideals of humanity in order to excavate and manifest

The light within.

Touch, my child

Your heart and the heart of others

With empathy, compassion, joy and peace

But most of all, with unconditional, boundless love

Because it is there that darkness cannot exist

And that negativity cannot grow

And that bullies cannot thrive

Love is the source of the light within

And the best teacher to us all

For no education is complete

No lesson is truly learned until we seek and find and embrace and treasure

The light within.

Know, my child

That in your soul, can be found your potential

From Latin, "potent", to be able and also from "potentia", power

Roots of words, roots of being that manifest

All of your power,

All the I CANs

That flow through the essence of I AM because of

The light within.

Be, my child

With every seed of authenticity

All the warm, fuzzy feelings of home within you

All that you are, all that sets you free

For it is in this freedom of being

In the presence of your True Self

That you will find your path, your purpose

And the infinite, inextinguishable True Spirit we know as

The light within.

AFTERWORD
Lessons learned

What sparks your soul? Write your answer within the flame in the illustration below. If you feel lost, return to that spark and let the light of your soul shine brightly for yourself and others.

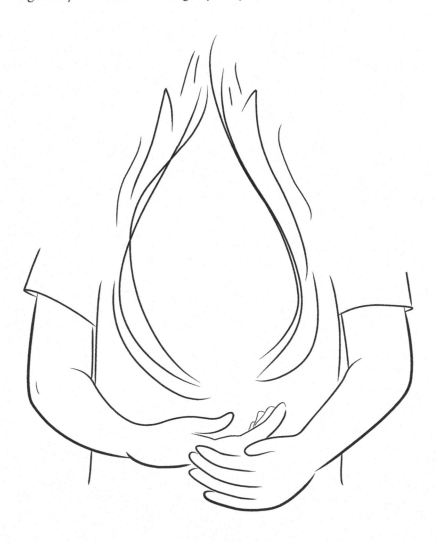